**I WON'T BE COMING
INTO WORK TODAY
BECAUSE YOU'RE
ALL DICKHEADS**

491/500

Copyright © David Thorne 2019 All rights reserved.

ISBN 978-0-9886895-7-2
I Won't Be Coming Into Work Today Because You're All Dickheads

www.27bslash6.com

This book is sold subject to the condition that it shall not, by way of trade or otherwise, be lent, re-sold, hired out, re-produced on the internet or otherwise circulated without the author's prior consent in any form of binding or cover other than that in which it is published and without a similar condition including this condition being imposed on the subsequent purchaser. Activities and vehicle modifications appearing or described in this book may be potentially dangerous.

By the same author:

The Internet is a Playground
The *New York Times* bestselling first release by David Thorne featuring articles from 27bslash6 plus over 160 pages of new material.

I'll Go Home Then; It's Warm and Has Chairs
The second collection of all new essays and emails.

Look Evelyn, Duck Dynasty Wiper Blades, We Should Get Them
The third collection of new essays and emails.

That's Not How You Wash a Squirrel
The fourth collection of new essays and emails.

Wrap It In a Bit of Cheese Like You're Tricking the Dog
The fifth collection of new essays and emails.

Walk It Off, Princess
The sixth collection of new essays and emails.

For Ben

A percentage of the profits from the sale of this book go towards Ben's Progeria treatments. He says he doesn't have Progeria but he wouldn't look the way he does if this were true. I'll probably buy him a beanie or something. I'm not spending more than $10 though.

Reviews

★☆☆☆☆ "Definitely the last book by David Thorne I'm ever buying. It's just a bunch of office related articles taken from his previous books and I've read all those. I get that it's an Australian release only but his previous books are available in Australia so I call bullshit."
Jim McPartland

★☆☆☆☆ "Shipping took eighteen weeks and it wasn't even the book I ordered."
Anne M. Thorson

★☆☆☆☆ "There isn't even a word for how disappointed I am. I'd need to use some kind of a chart."
Michele Wagner

★☆☆☆☆ "Is this meant to be some kind of a 'best of' book? Because it isn't. My face was exactly like the sheep on the cover when I flipped through it."
David C. Little

★☆☆☆☆ "How is this a guide? A guide has steps to take with examples and maybe illustrations. This isn't a guide. I don't know what it is. I better win a grappling hook."
Jarvis McLimans

Contents

Introduction 9

David & His Best Friends at the Office 14

A Stone in a Teacup 17

David's Bin 19

Ben's Shirt 20

You Look Like You're 21

Things Simon Said This Week That Annoyed Me 25

Cabbages 27

Average length of Kenneth's meetings (in hours) 2.8

Answering Ben's Emails 42

Amount of items in this contents list 44

Ten Emails From Walter That Make No Sense 52

People who know how to use a spiral binder 0

Silhouettes of Simon Giving Oral to Things 56

Ten Formal Complaints 57

Timesheets 77

Team Building 91

E34-F 99

Terrabytes of porn on Ben's computer 6

More Branded 105

Interviews	117
Product Naming	129
Kenneth's Meetings	130
Kenneth's Horns	139
Production Meeting	140
Missing Missy	170
Fire	185
Tom's Diary	186
Cloud Backgrounds	195
Jumping Frog Fee	207
Kevin's Party	216
Walter's Dyslexia	B
Telephones and Apps	217
Charlie	228
Aaaaaron's Bank Account Balance	$1.87
Kevin's Retorts	238
Kevin's Office	240
Ben's Car	244
Quick Logo	247
Photography	249
Who's Pat?	258
One Girl, Twelve Cups	271
Simon's Pie Charts	277
Just a Sandwich, Thanks	288

Introduction

The branding agency I work for fired a junior graphic designer named Aaaaaron last month. I realize I may have added too many A's to Aaaaaron's name but there were too many to begin with and it's easier to just hold down the A key for a bit than remember the correct number. I assume Aaaaaron's parents wanted him to be first on lists or something but if that's the case, Aardvark would have done.

Mike, our Creative Director, had me break the news to Aaaaaron as Mike avoids confrontation. Once, when an angry client turned up unexpectedly with his lawyer, I watched from my office window as Mike jumped the back fence and ran down an alley. Twelve-thousand brochures for landscaping services had been printed and mailed out with the caption under a photo of guy pruning a hedge stating, "Ben hasn't supplied text for this yet. Please inform the useless cunt he has 2 days before this goes to print."

Aaaaaron wasn't very good at his job and he smelled like milk that has been left in a vehicle for a few weeks during summer. Someone once told me that this is how all Caucasians smell to Asians, because Asians don't drink milk, but I asked my Asian friend Brian if this was true and he replied, "No, we drink milk, dickhead. Who told you that?"

Aaaaaron didn't take the news of his dismissal well. He'd signed a lease on an apartment close to the agency and bought expensive boots the day before.

"You can't fire me. I have a contract."
"Yes, which states in the first paragraph that you're on a three month trial period. You've been here less than two weeks."
"I just rented an apartment. And I bought these boots yesterday. They're Frye."
"Frye make men's boots?"
"Yes."
"Nice. Did you keep the receipt?"
"No."
"Pity, you could have taken them back. Got yourself a pair of Hush Puppies instead."
"You think this a joke? How am I meant to pay my rent?"
"Perhaps you should have thought about that before you lied on your résumé."
"That doesn't make any sense, I wrote my résumé six months ago. And I didn't lie on it."
"It states you're proficient in Illustrator."
"So?"
"You took an hour to draw a circle this morning."
"And color it."
"Sure. Had you ever used Illustrator before starting here, Aaaaaron?"
"Yes. Well, FreeHand actually. It's a much better program than Illustrator."
"I agree. Freehand is far more intuitive. Unfortunately, its

last update was in 2003 and it won't run on computers manufactured after 2011. What about Photoshop?"

"I never said I was proficient at Photoshop."

"No, you said you were 'adept'."

"Adept isn't as good as proficient."

"Taking two days to turn an image to grayscale is hardly adept. A five-year-old could have Googled how to do it in ten minutes. Have you ever used Google, Aaaaaron?"

"Fuck you."

"Sorry?

Fuck you. I was going to quit anyway. This job sucks and you're all a bunch of pretentious wankers."

"Right, well that works out perfectly for everyone then. We accept your resignation. All the best with your future endeavors and let me know if you need a reference."

"You're going to be seriously fucking sorry."

"I already am, Aaaaaron. Still, live and learn; we'll probably make your replacement do some kind of test to make sure they didn't just Google 'what programs do graphic designers use?' for their resume."

"You'll see."

Aaaaaron kicked the photocopier on his way out of the boardroom. It was a decent kick and dented a panel so we'll have to get that replaced. The kick also left a decent scuff on Aaaaaron's right Frye boot, so there's no way he's going to be able to return them, and he may have broken a toe because he made a weird surprised face and shook his hands up and down as if he was having a seizure before limping upstairs to collect his stuff. Graphic designers can be rather melodramatic at times.

We assumed the photocopier attack was the extent of Aaaaaron's revenge but he returned at 1.17am that night with a brick. We know it was 1.17am because the security video is timestamped. The footage showed Aaaaaron pulling his purple Kia Soul up outside the office, with his number plate clearly visible, and attempting to throw the brick without getting out of his car. The brick made the distance but it mustn't have had much momentum as it bounced off the window. Aaaaaron had to open his car door and get out to retrieve the brick and he put some real effort into his second throw; the glass shattered and the alarm sounded. I've set the alarm off by accident before and the pitch, volume, and strobe lighting made my legs go wobbly. I guess Aaaaaron hadn't anticipated the alarm as he made the same face and hand thing he'd done when he kicked the photocopier, and ran off - apparently forgetting that he'd driven. He returned a few minutes later, sprinting into view and practically dived into his car - striking his head on the roof as he did so. There was no sound in the footage but it must have made a decent 'dong'. Possibly stunned by the blow, Aaaaaron put his car into reverse, with the door still open, and slammed the accelerator. The door hit a No Parking sign and bent backwards - it must have damaged the hinges because Aaaaaron had to get out and kick it to get it closed. He couldn't open it again so he ran around to the passenger side and climbed through before driving off.

Mike and I watched the footage in his office the next morning. We chuckled when the brick bounced off the window but were in tears by the time Aaaaaron made his getaway. Other staff members made their way in to see what the howls were about and we rewatched the footage probably thirty times. Somehow it became funnier with each viewing and at one point Mike had to lay on the floor because he couldn't breathe. We'd initially intended to notify the police but agreed that the entertainment was worth the inconvenience of having the window replaced and that Aaaaaron had enough issues to deal with without being arrested. Besides, he wasn't wrong; we are all pretentious wankers and working here does suck. It probably sucks less than being homeless and unemployed with a broken toe and concussion and having to climb across the passenger seat to get into a Kia Soul though.

I saw Aaaaaron in a supermarket a week or so later. He was buying bananas and pancake mix and had a large purple bruise with stitches on his forehead. I was a few people behind him in the checkout queue but he saw me. He pretended he hadn't but his face went red and sweaty and the checkout girl asked him if he was okay. He said he was so that's good. His card was declined though.

David & His Best Friends at the Office

A Stone in a Teacup

"Jodie is such a massive bitch."
"Why, Walter, what did you do?"
"Why do you assume I did something?"
"You only ever call Melissa a bitch when she tells you off about something."
"That's not true, I called her a bitch yesterday when she commented on what I was wearing. What business is it of hers if my t-shirt and shorts are the same color? It's called color coordination."
"It did kind of look like you were wearing a romper."
"What's a romper?"
"It's like a jumpsuit but with shorts. The matching belt didn't help."
"My shirt was untucked most of the day, I only tucked it in because I had a client meeting."
"Fair enough. Better to look like a 1976 JC Penney catalogue model than unkempt. What is Jodie being a bitch about today?"
"Nothing. That's the point. She's just putting a stone in a teacup."
"Sorry?"
"Who cares if you rinse and squeeze out a sponge after you use it or not? You rinse it and squeeze it out before you use it anyway."

"The phrase is a 'storm' in a teacup, Walter."

"No it isn't. Why would there be a storm in a teacup?"

"It's an idiom meaning a small event that has been exaggerated out of proportion. Why would anyone put a stone in a teacup? It doesn't make any sense."

"It makes more sense than a storm in a teacup. Cups don't have wind or clouds but anyone can put a stone in one."

"Granted, but why would they?"

"Say you've got a cup of tea, and it's full to the top. Everything is fine and you're about to enjoy your cup of tea and then someone puts a stone in it and it overflows."

"Because you didn't rinse out a sponge?"

"Exactly."

"So your take on the phrase is vengeful displacement?"

"It doesn't matter where it's placed, if the cup is full and you add a stone, it's going to spill everywhere. People like Jodie who put stones in teacups are just creating issues for no reason. She's not the boss of the kitchen. She's not the boss of anything. She needs to get out of her high house."

David's Bin

I heard Jodie fart this morning. I actually heard her fart three times - four if you count the little squeak at the end as she made a final check.

She hadn't seen me when she walked upstairs and sat at her desk - I was under Walter's desk, stealing a laptop cable. I popped my head up when I heard the first fart, it was like one of those fake ones you make by licking your arm and giving it a raspberry, one with a lot of spit. Her back was to me and I watched as she lifted her left cheek and farted again. The first must have been a test run because the second ran for triple the time and at a much lower pitch. It was like a drawn out sigh mixed with the sound of a flag flapping in a strong breeze. The third was shorter, softer, and faded out like a librarian saying 'shhhhh'. The fourth, as mentioned, was just a small squeak - or like that water-drop noise some people can make by flicking their cheek.

At the sound of someone walking up the stairs, Jodie quickly wafted the air behind her with a hand. Mike stepped off the landing and made a face.
"Jesus fucking Christ, what's that smell?" he asked.
"I know," Jodie replied, nodding and making a distasteful face, "I smelled it when I came up. I think it's David's bin."

Ben's Shirt

Ben bought a new shirt on the weekend. He wore it to work Monday and flitted gaily in and out of people's offices all morning for us to admire. It looked like any other shirt, perhaps a little shinier because of the cotton/nylon blend, but it wasn't like any other shirt; it was the best shirt in the world. It hadn't been advertised as such but Ben had suspected the shirt was the best shirt in the world the moment he saw it in on the rack. When he tried it on in the changing room, he knew it was. The points on the collar were extra sharp and the collar itself was slightly lower than usual. It also had the second to top button in the correct place; not so high that it looked silly when done up and not so low that it showed chest hair when left undone. It was light blue, bordering on grey-blue. The kind of grey-blue that looks great with either a suit or jeans. He'd worn it tucked in that day but it looked equally as good untucked, it was the perfect length for either. Ninety-five dollars was expensive for a shirt but not for the best shirt in the world. Besides, he'd received ten percent off for signing up for a department store credit card.

"New shirt?" asked Mike.
"Yes," replied Ben, beaming, "it's John Varvatos."
"It's very shiny. You look like you're on your way to a disco."

You Look Like You're

"You look like you're" is Mike's way of saying, "I wouldn't be caught dead in that and here's a thinly disguised insult to explain why." Apparently he's not even aware he's being insulting so maybe it's just something gay men have built in, like the ability to hold their breath under water for a long time. I asked him last week why he couldn't just compliment someone on their attire without using the term, "You look like you're," and he replied, "I've never said that in my life, I'm full of compliments."

As such, I decided to record every time Mike said "You look like you're," over a five day period:

Monday, 10.35am, David's boots.

"New boots?"
"Yes, I ordered them from the Sundance catalogue."
"They look comfy."
"They are."
"You look like you're going for a hike."
"What's that supposed to mean?"
"Nothing, they're very rural, that's all. You know what would go well with those boots?"
"What?"
"A walking staff."

Monday, 12.02pm, Walter's beige cargo shorts

"New cargo shorts, Walter?"
"No, I don't think I've worn these to work before though."
"They're very 'safari'. You look like you're about to wrestle a warthog or point out a giraffe in the distance."

Monday, 3.41pm, Kevin's sweater

"Did your wife knit you a new sweater, Kevin?"
"This? No, it's from JC Penny."
"Cosy. You look like you're about to go crab fishing or take your border collie for a walk across the misty Scottish highlands."

Tuesday, 9.14am, Melissa's yellow dress

"Morning Melissa, is that a new dress?"
"Fairly new."
"It's very floral. You look like you're on your way to a country barn dance or to sell jam at a fair from the back of a pickup truck."

Tuesday, 11.04am, Jennifer's blouse

"New top, Jen?"
"It's a blouse."
"You look like you're about to teach a painting class."
"I don't give a fuck what you think, Mike."
"Jesus, learn to take a compliment, Jen."

Wednesday, 9.19am, Jodie's 'Sia' haircut

"Looks like someone's had a haircut."
"Yes, it's a bit short and I've never had bangs before but I thought I'd try something a bit more modern."
"It's certainly modern. You look like you're on your way to join the crew of the USS Enterprise. Beam me up, Doctor Spock."
"It's *Mister* Spock, Doctor Spock wrote books on parenting."
"Nobody cares, Space Bob."

Wednesday, 2.24pm, David's black jacket

"Superdry?"
"It's a British clothing brand."
"Yes, I'm aware of the brand, I just didn't know anyone was still wearing it. You look like you're on a night operation as part of a special ops military team."
"Good, that's exactly what I was going for."
"Apart from your physique of course. They'd never let you in. You're too old."

Thursday 9.12am, Melissa's necklace

"That's an interesting necklace, Melissa."
"Thanks, my sister brought it back for me from her trip to Mexico."
"It's Mexican? I would have guessed African. You look like you're on your way to a neighbouring village to be swapped for two cows and a goat-hide water pouch."

Thursday, 4.32pm, Ben's beard

"Are you growing a beard?"
"I thought I'd see how it looks. It hasn't grown in yet."
"Yes, it just looks like you've been camping for a few days. Are you going to grow it all over or just on the chin?"
"All over."
"Good. You look like that stoner guy in Scooby Doo at the moment."
"Shaggy?"
"No, not the dog, the guy that owns the dog."

Friday 9.16am, Walter's grey suit

"Why are you in a suit?"
"I have a funeral to go to at twelve o'clock today."
"You don't own a better suit than that? One that fits? You look like you're on the way to a Salvation Army men's shelter for free soup. Who's the funeral for?"
"My dad. It's one of his suits."
"Right, well grab your phone and let Melissa know we're going out for an hour."
"Why? Where are we going?"
"A store I like. I'm going to buy you a new suit."

Things Simon Said This Week That Annoyed Me

"Most people would die within a few days if they were lost in the wilderness. Not me though. I would build a paddle wheel generator in a creek and protect my campsite with an electric fence."

"David should have to wear a tie to work. I wear a tie every day. It means you take pride in your appearance and care about what other people think about you. Like when you meet an african elder and place your spear on the ground. It's a sign of respect."

"I just went to make a coffee and there are no k-cups left for the Keurig. We had a box of 50 and I counted the used ones in the bin and there are 16 missing. David has a Keurig at home so I think we should be allowed to check his bag each day before he leaves."

"That thing about only being able to fold a piece of paper eight times is rubbish. Give me a piece of paper the size of a bed sheet and an industrial metal press, and I could easily double that."

"I could build a robot with artificial intelligence if I wanted to - if you gave me enough money and a year or two. I pick things up pretty quickly and I have a huge shed."

"When I have kids, they won't be allowed to watch television. They can watch the news but that's it. My kids will be highly intelligent and if I let them waste that gift watching Family Guy, what kind of parent would that make me? They should be sculpting or learning the flute instead."

"Did you know that if you multiply 1089 x 9 you get 9801. It's reversed itself! It also works with 10989 or 109989 or 1099989 and so on."

"We should stagger our lunch breaks, and cut them down to fifteen minutes. That way we would each only be unproductive for a total of 75 minutes per week. I bring a packed lunch and eat it at my desk while I am working which means I am only unproductive for the time it takes me to wash my hands before and after."

"I read that underwear reduces your sperm count so I don't wear any. I don't want my kids to have Spina-bifida. There is no real point to underwear anyway when you think about it. I also only wear pants that have twenty percent or more lycra in the blend."

Cabbages

There's a small island off the southern tip of the Great Andaman archipelago, shaped a bit like a slice of bread, called North Sentinel Island. Nobody knows what the people living on North Sentinel Island call the island because the inhabitants, noted for resisting all attempts at contact by outsiders, are more interested in throwing spears than chatting.

They maintain a society subsisting through hunting, fishing, and collecting wild plants. There is no evidence of either agricultural practices or methods of producing fire and their language remains unknown.

Every twenty years or so, anthropologists attempt to coax the islanders from their hostile reception of outsiders by leaving coconuts on the beach and waving from boats anchored just beyond spear-throwing distance. Sometimes the natives wave back and the anthropologists, encouraged, approach close enough to be speared.

Which is why I call my desk North Sentinel Island II.

I made my own flag, by drawing a pair of crossed spears on a blank timesheet, and flew it from my desk using sticky-tape and a ruler.

"What's the X stand for?" asked Kevin.

Kevin, an account manager at the design agency I work for, makes regular attempts at contact with North Sentinel Island II but instead of offering coconuts, he offers lengthy tales of how well his cabbages are growing and the soil conditions required for such.

"It's not an X," I informed him, "It's two spears crossing over each other."

I've never been overly adept at drawing. It might be assumed that some degree of artistic aptitude is required to work in the design industry but there's a vast difference between pencil on paper and pixels on screen. I can split paths and know the names of far too many typefaces, but I'd be the last person I'd pick as a partner on Pictionary night.

"Is it a person rollerskating during a tornado?"
"No, it's a grape."

When I was nine, I drew a picture in class of my dog Gus jumping into a pond. The teacher mistook it for an excellent picture of a snake coming out of a cave and I was elected to participate in the painting of a school mural depicting wildlife preservation. Featured in the school corridor for the next four years, between fairly decent representations of an ostrich and elephant by students with a modicum of talent, was what became known as *David's egg-flip with eyes*.

"It looks more like an X," Kevin critiqued, "If you made the pointy bits more profound, like they were made out of sharpened rocks, and added bits of cloth hanging down where the rocks are tied to the sticks, they would look a lot more like spears."

"Right, thank you for the suggestion, Kevin. I should probably have consulted you on correct spear drawing techniques prior to undertaking the design. What can I help you with?"

"Nothing," he replied, scrolling through his iPhone, "I just wanted to show you something..."

"Is it a photo of a cabbage?" I asked, "I've already seen it."

"No, hang on... wait, that's not it... that's my daughter's eldest at his graduation ceremony, nice kid, top marks in his class... hang on... I know it's here somewhere..."

"I'm fairly busy at the moment..." I tried interjecting.

"Here it is... no, wait, that's not it either..."

I tried growing my own vegetables once, after watching a program called *Preppers* in which people with beards and Wrangler jeans anticipate social collapse. I paid around $30 for seeds, $100 for railway ties, and $250 for fifty bags of garden soil which means the two cucumbers I ended up with cost $190 each. They weren't even good cucumbers. One was about two inches in length and the other had a huge grub living inside it.

Should the grid ever 'go down', I estimate my chances of long-term survival as slim at best. I'll probably be shot at the supermarket and have my cans of evaporated milk and instant coffee taken from me on the first day.

My coworker Simon once told me that he really wished there would be a zombie apocalypse like in the show, *The Walking Dead*.
"I'd use a bow, or crossbow," he said, "Like Darryl. Because it's quieter."
"Sure," I agreed, "But the reload is dreadful. You'd probably be better off with a shotgun. Even if it is a bit louder. You don't have to be a very good aim with a shotgun."
Simon smiled and shook his head, "That's why I'd be a main character and you'd be one of the new people that joins our community then gets bitten and turns into a zombie that I have to shoot. With an arrow."

When I was ten, I shot my dog Gus with an arrow. It wasn't on purpose though and he didn't die or anything. He just ran around the yard yelping with the arrow in his hind leg for a bit until my mother came out to see what all the noise was about. I'd built the bow out of a branch and packaging twine. Lacking actual feathers to use as stabilisers for the arrows, I attached a leaf to the end of a fairly straight stick with tape, and sharpened the other end. Upon testing, I found it almost impossible to draw back the taught string, so I laid on my back, placed both feet in the bow with the arrow between, and pulled with both hands.

With my arms and legs quivering from the strain and the string cutting deep into my fingers, I aimed towards a box sitting on top of a stump. The box had concentric circles drawn on it but instead of giving each a number, I'd written the names of all the people in my class who called me by the nickname 'Egg-flip'. With my bent knees about to give out, I pushed just a bit a harder... and my legs locked straight up, ripping the string from my grip. Due to the high angle of trajectory, the arrow travelled perhaps sixty feet in height but only twenty in distance. Gus was lying on his side on the grass, enjoying the sun, when the arrow hit.

I wasn't punished by my parents for the incident but I did have to listen to the "We're not angry, we're just disappointed" speech. My parents were never really big on discipline. The only physical punishment I remember receiving was having my mouth washed out with soap. I was seven. My father switched channels to the news while I was watching *The Goodies* and, having heard a term that day at school and assuming it was a generic one like ragamuffin or boofhead, I called him a cocksucker.

Dragged down the hallway and into the bathroom, what I recall of the punishment was not the taste of the soap, but the fact that the only bar available was a mushy blob stuck to the tiled floor of the shower. As I spat the soap, and a toenail, into the sink afterwards, I remember thinking, 'Nobody in our family has short curly hair, whose hair is this?'

I mentioned the the soap incident to my father a few years back and he said, "Bullshit. It was Brut-33 soap-on-a-rope. It was hanging on the tap. That's what the rope is for you fucking liar."

As my father wasn't a fan of vet bills, he bandaged Gus' leg with duct tape and, to stop Gus gnawing at it, duct taped an old lampshade to his head as a makeshift cone. Gus walked with a limp for the rest of his life. Which wasn't very long as he was hit by a car a week later. Either he couldn't hobble out of the way in time or simply didn't see the car as the lampshade was pretty big and had tassels. We buried him in the backyard but my father dug him up a few months later when we put in a pool. He still had the duct tape on his hind leg and a note under his collar that read, "Dear Gus, Sorry for shooting you in the leg with an arrow. You were a good dog. Except when you stood in front of the TV."

"Ah, here it is!" declared Kevin finally. He held up the screen to show me a photo of a cabbage.
"You showed me that yesterday," I remarked, "and I told you at the time that if I wanted to look at pictures of cabbages I'd type 'pictures of cabbages' into Google."
"It's a different photo," he explained, "look how much they've grown in just a few days."
A photo of a cabbage growing in soil, without something in the photo for scale, such as a banana, could be two inches or two feet across. I pointed this out to Kevin.

Kevin looked at the photo and frowned, "You're a fucking idiot," he said on his way out.

After he left, I made the pointy bits on my flag look like sharpened rocks and added bits of cloth where they were joined the sticks. It did actually look better but then I tried adding blood to the end of the spears with a red whiteboard marker which made the spears look like match sticks wearing ties so I had to redo the entire thing.

The phone on my desk rang.

"North Sentinel Island II tourist information. This is David. How can I help you?"
"What?" Melissa asked, "Is Kevin up there? Ben's on hold for him."

Melissa replaced our previous secretary - or 'front desk manager' as Sharon had preferred to be called - a few years back after what is commonly referred to as the Recipient Incident.

Mistakenly selecting 'Staff' instead of her boyfriend 'Steve', Sharon sent a selfie of herself wearing only pigtails to everyone in the office. Being fat - or 'curvy' as fat people prefer to be called - the thing that impressed me most about the selfie was her flexibility. There's no way I could get my feet behind my head, even with a pillow under my back like she had. I've tried.

While I can understand Sharon's decision to leave without notice, the subject matter was actually less embarrassing than the environment the photo was taken in. Her bedroom had green striped wallpaper and a ruffled floral bedspread. A stained glass lamp shaped like a butterfly was just visible amongst a throng of teddy bears on her side table and above her bed was a poster of a tiger. Who lives like this? If it was my bedroom, I wouldn't be taking nude selfies, I would be weeping as I splashed kerosene about and lit a match.

I was actually glad when she left. The only bathroom is across the hall from my office and Sharon apparently suffered from Irritable Bowel Syndrome. It wasn't the noise, which was like twenty sauce bottles being simultaneously squeezed to the last drop, but the fact that she would leave the door open after finishing. Almost every time, I would have to get up, walk through her Agent-Orange-like mist, and close the door.

"Can we try keeping this door closed please?" I once asked.
"Sorry," Sharon replied sarcastically.
"Yes, I don't think you are actually sorry otherwise you'd close the door and not subject everyone to what smells like a large pile of dead cats. Dead cats covered in shit. The 'Fresh Linen' Febreeze doesn't mask the odour, it just makes it smell like a large pile of dead cats covered in shit with a dryer-sheet stuck on top."
"You're so rude," she replied, "I can't help it if I have Irritable Bowel Syndrome. It's a medical condition."

From: Jennifer Haines
To: David Thorne
Subject: Complaint

David,

Sharon has filed a F26-A in regards to comments you allegedly made about a medical condition she suffers from. Under section 3, paragraph 8 of the Employee Workplace Agreement it states that no employee will be discriminated against for any medical condition. Please keep your opinions to yourself in future. Irritable Bowel Syndrome is a real condition.

Jennifer

....

From: David Thorne
To: Jennifer Haines
Subject: Re: Complaint

Jennifer,

I'm sure it is but if I were to bother looking up the symptoms, I doubt they would include an inability to close doors.

Besides, I'm fairly sure dropping the fecal equivalent of Hiroshima every few hours has more to do with diet than disorders. I once saw her eat a cake for lunch. Not a cupcake or a large slice of cake, a whole cake. If someone of normal weight defecated with the regularity and magnitude of Sharon's seismic dumps, they would be dead within the day. It would be like an average sized dog giving birth to a cow.

Regards, David

"No," I answered Melissa, "I think Kevin went out."
'Right." Click.

This was pretty much the extent of Melissa's phone etiquette. She hadn't been employed based on experience. Despite a sign on the front window stating, 'No Soliciting', various people often enter off the street asking if anyone wants to buy things from a big bag. The items are usually cheap electronics, memo holders, flashlight keychains. That sort of thing. I like it when they come in. The day after Sharon left, a girl in her early twenties came in lugging her bag of wares. It was raining outside and she looked miserable.

"Hello, my name is Melissa and I was wondering if anyone in this office would be interested in purchasing items from a fabulous selection of fabulous gifts and gadgets?"
"Do they make you say that?" I asked.
"Yes."
"You said the word fabulous twice. Was it supposed to be 'a fabulous selection' or 'fabulous gifts and gadgets'?"

"Fabulous gifts and gadgets," she answered, "It's my first day."
"How's it working out? Are you selling lots of gifts and gadgets?"
"No."
"Do you want a better job?"

She doesn't have to do much. Apart from answering and redirecting the occasional incoming call, she mainly just sits at her desk flicking between Facebook and Twitter. Once, while presenting to a client, I popped my head out to ask if she'd mind making coffees and she tweeted, "OMG, idiot at work just told me to make coffee. #imnotyourfuckingslave #spit."

I didn't see the tweet until after the presentation so I'm fairly sure I drank coffee with spit in it.

....

From: Jennifer Haines
To: David Thorne
Subject: Melissa

David,

All staff recruitment is to be approved by the HR department. Under no circumstances do you have authority to offer anyone a position here.

Melissa has zero experience, zero qualifications, and zero knowledge of the position. Furthermore, she is not your cousin and the entire story about her parents dying in a fire was fabricated. I've spoken to her and she knows nothing about it. She has been given a trial period but do not let this happen again.

Jennifer

....

The phone rang again.
"Ben wants to speak to you." said Melissa, "He's on line 3."
Click.

"Hurro? Mr Moshiyoto?" I said in an old Asian woman's voice as per procedure. I can't recall why Ben and I started doing this but it would be weird to start answering the phone normally now.
"Terrible," said Ben, "That sounded more like a Mexican man with emphysema than an Asian woman. Hey, I was just wondering, do you like the band Linkin Park?"

When a client is given a timeline for project completion of, say, three weeks, this does not mean the project takes three weeks to complete. It means somewhere between looking at photos of cabbages, closing bathroom doors, discussing weapons of choice during a zombie apocalypse, answering phone calls, making your own coffee and drawing flags, a few hours will be spent quickly throwing their project together. Often those few hours will be allocated to the few hours before the client arrives to view what you have been working on for three weeks.

I once designed a logo while a client waited in the foyer. Melissa entertained them with an explanation of why she chose to wear boots with leggings rather than boots with a dress that day while I turned an 8 sideways to make an infinity symbol, chopped a bit out of one of the loops, and turned it orange. The new logo was presented ten minutes later to the client, a large financial investment company, as "a graphic representation of koi which are symbolic of wealth in Japanese culture."

"It's beautiful. Simple yet balanced, solid yet flowing. I also love the typeface you used for our name, what's it called?"
"Helvetica."
"Just stunning."

A few years before, while working for an Australian design agency called De Masi Jones, I was commissioned to come up with a new name and branding for a flight training company. Forgetting about the project until the day due, they were presented with the name 'Altara' and told it was an aboriginal word, from the Boonjari tribe, meaning 'above the clouds'. The client was happy and Altara is now an established brand in the aeronautics industry. There is no such thing as the Boonjari tribe.

While it is entirely possible that spending time allocated to a project on the actual project might produce a better result, it's a scenario I have no experience with or expectations of.

"We charged the client for 132 hours, how many hours were spent?"
"132"
"Oh no, what happened? We will never make money like that."
"I'm kidding, it was 2."
"Thank god. By the way, have I shown you my new golf clubs? I'll bring them upstairs to your office and demonstrate club selection, stance, swing and follow-through even though you have no interest in the subject. Kevin, would you like to join me? While I'm setting up a makeshift putting green, you can explain to David the importance of good soil drainage."

Kevin returned a short time later and made his way into my office.
"The spears look better," he commented, "one's a bit bent though. It wouldn't be very aerodynamic."
"What can I help you with, Kevin?"
"I just want to show you something," he replied, taking out his iPhone.
"Fantastic, I hope it's a photo of cabbage."
"Look... no, that's not... here it is!"

The photo showed Kevin, down on one knee, holding a measuring tape across the top of a cabbage.

"Eleven and a half inches," he proclaimed proudly, "The key is making sure the soil has a pH balance between 6.5 and 7.5."

Answering Ben's Emails For Him While He's Out For The Afternoon

From: Margaret Harper
Date: Thursday 9 June 2016 11.43am
To: Ben Townsend
Subject: Flyer changes

Hey,

Are you able do the Barry thing this afternoon?

Maggie

From: Ben Townsend
Date: Thursday 9 June 2016 12.06pm
To: Margaret Harper
Subject: Re: Flyer changes

No, but I can do saults.

From: Margaret Harper
Date: Thursday 9 June 2016 12.14pm
To: Ben Townsend
Subject: Re: Re: Flyer changes

What's saults?

Maggie

....

From: Ben Townsend
Date: Thursday 9 June 2016 12.17pm
To: Margaret Harper
Subject: Re: Re: Re: Flyer changes

Somersaults.

....

From: Robert Dawson
Date: Thursday 9 June 2016 12.03pm
To: Ben Townsend
Subject: Re: Business card layout

Ben, they like the layout but can you make the font a bit bigger (the target audience is retirement age) and change the border to blue?

Thank you, Rob

From: Ben Townsend
Date: Thursday 9 June 2016 12.22pm
To: Robert Dawson
Subject: Re: Re: Business card layout

Hello Rob,

I can certainly make the changes but as we are well over-budget on this project, I will have to charge $12,000 as additional.

Ben

From: Robert Dawson
Date: Thursday 9 June 2016 12.29pm
To: Ben Townsend
Subject: Re: Re: Re: Business card layout

I hope that's a typo. Why would it cost that much?

From: Ben Townsend
Date: Thursday 9 June 2016 12.32pm
To: Robert Dawson
Subject: Re: Re: Re: Re: Business card layout

I'm thinking about buying a boat.

From: Melissa Peters
Date: Thursday 9 June 2016 11.51am
To: Ben Townsend
Subject: Client briefing

Jeff rang. He said the meeting is at 3 today. Do you know where his office is?

From: Ben Townsend
Date: Thursday 9 June 2016 12.12pm
To: Melissa Peters
Subject: Re: Client briefing

Do I look like a compass?

From: Jason Greene
Date: Thursday 9 June 2016 12.37pm
To: Ben Townsend
Subject: Meeting Friday

Hi Ben

Do you need me to arrange a projector for tomorrow or do you have your own for the presentation?

Jason

From: Ben Townsend
Date: Thursday 9 June 2016 12.43pm
To: Jason Greene
Subject: Re: Meeting Friday

Hello Jason,

A projector won't be necessary as I intend to present the packaging concepts through cosplay. As such, I might need to change the meeting to next week, as my mother hasn't finished sewing my costume yet.

Ben

From: Jason Greene
Date: Thursday 9 June 2016 12.47pm
To: Ben Townsend
Subject: Re: Re: Meeting Friday

Are you serious?

From: Ben Townsend
Date: Thursday 9 June 2016 12.52pm
To: Jason Greene
Subject: Re: Re: Re: Meeting Friday

I know right? She doesn't understand that people have deadlines to meet.

From: Kevin Eastwood
Date: Thursday 9 June 2016 12.11pm
To: Ben Townsend
Subject: Walker copy

How are we going on the Purina project? They were expecting to see revised copy today. What do you want me to tell them?

Kevin

....

From: Ben Townsend
Date: Thursday 9 June 2016 12.15pm
To: Kevin Eastwood
Subject: Re: Walker copy

Tell them the copy is exactly the same as the previous version but I've replaced every eighth word with a photo of the Hubble telescope as requested.

....

From: Kevin Eastwood
Date: Thursday 9 June 2016 12.20pm
To: Ben Townsend
Subject: Re: Re: Walker copy

Nobody requested that.

From: Lauren Townsend
Date: Thursday 9 June 2016 11.48pm
To: Ben Townsend
CC: Jamie Townsend, Sarah Townsend
Subject: Moms birthday <3

Hi, I looked at prices on the new Kindle and if all 4 of us put in, it's $35 each. If that's ok I'll order it tonight. x

Lauren

....

From: Ben Townsend
Date: Thursday 9 June 2016 12.36pm
To: Lauren Townsend
CC: Jamie Townsend, Sarah Townsend, Janet Lynch
Subject: Re: Moms birthday <3

Bit steep for me. You guys go thirds, I'll make her a mixtape.

....

From: Graham Sullivan
Date: Thursday 9 June 2016 12.34pm
To: Ben Townsend
Subject: Bowling

Sorry about Saturday. I forgot I promised Vicky I'd help her move. Still friends? :)

From: Ben Townsend
Date: Thursday 9 June 2016 12.34pm
To: Graham Sullivan
Subject: Re: Bowling

I promise no matter what, I will never be your friend and I will hate you for the rest of my life.

....

From: Evan Manning
Date: Thursday 9 June 2016 12.12pm
To: Ben Townsend
Subject: June crossfit fun run

I'm picking up the t-shirts today. What size do you want?
Evan

....

From: Ben Townsend
Date: Thursday 9 June 2016 12.19pm
To: Evan Manning
Subject: Re: June crossfit fun run

3XL please. I like them baggy.

From: Aisha Gaddafi
Date: Thursday 9 June 2016 10.06am
To: Ben Townsend
Subject: Greetings from Aisha

Hello Dear,

Permit me to take your moment to inform you of my desire to go into relationship with you, as I have prayed, and I need a trust-worthy person in my project. I am the daughter of the Late President of Libya, Late President Muammar Gaddafi. I don't want many people to know about me because of my position and my family popularity, as such, please treat this letter very confidential. I don't want to involve any other person in this matter please. I want to trust you and you alone. Thanks.

Before my father died, part of the valuables he secured which I have the details, is Gold of great value, worth $750,000,000.00. After the death of my father, I quickly ran to Algeria. When, I got to Algeria, I was not feeling very safe and secured, so I wrote to the United Nations and they took me to Oman Muscat. I herein solicit for your kind assistance of funds for a plane ticket to fly to your country so that you may help me invest this money. I will give you 30% for your efforts. I join you in your country soon to live comfortably and invest.

Thank you and May God bless you.

Aisha Gaddafi

From: Ben Townsend
Date: Thursday 9 June 2016 12.49pm
To: Aisha Gaddafi
Subject: Re: Greetings from Aisha

Dear Aisha,

I'm very sorry to hear of your troubles and of course I will do anything to help. Please find my credit card details below.

This card has a high interest rate so please don't buy anything but the plane tickets.

Let me know when you're on your way.

Ben

BEN C TOWNSEND
VISA 4147 2022 4835 2398 Exp. 04/19
(CVV 813)

Ten Emails From Walter That Make No Sense

From: Walter Bowers
Date: Thursday 10 September 2015 10.13am
To: David Thorne
Subject: No Subject

Bugs in your office. not bugs stinky beetles?

From: Walter Bowers
Date: Monday 28 September 2015 2.07pm
To: David Thorne
Subject: No Subject

Are you sweet i am. someone needs to batteries the air conditioner before we all suffocate. AAA. 2 of them.

From: Walter Bowers
Date: Wednesday 14 October 2015 9.26am
To: David Thorne
Subject: No Subject

Hear the engine in the water cooler?

From: Walter Bowers
Date: Monday 9 November 2015 3.11pm
To: David Thorne
Subject: No Subject

I forgot it was today. Can you they have m&ms and comfortable seats. You don't have to wait in the car. they have good magazines too. I might not go though. i'll let you know before 4

From: Walter Bowers
Date: Friday 20 November 2015 1.20pm
To: David Thorne
Subject: No Subject

Do I nod like its ok to Jodie if she says please instead of just telling people to do? Its just manners bitch.

From: Walter Bowers
Date: Thursday 3 December 2015 4.45pm
To: David Thorne
Subject: No Subject

19 12 64 2 14 3 18 6

From: Walter Bowers
Date: Monday 18 January 2016 9.22am
To: David Thorne
Subject: No Subject

From: Walter Bowers
Date: Wednesday 17 February 2016 11.43am
To: David Thorne
Subject: No Subject

That's what happens wet it gets wet then you get rust. Its easier to oil it before it gets clean the rust off. Not my problem anyway.

From: Walter Bowers
Date: Tuesday 8 March 2016 12.16pm
To: David Thorne
Subject: No Subject

Because angles.

....

From: Walter Bowers
Date: Wednesday 18 May 2016 4.01pm
To: David Thorne
Subject: No Subject

Nobody the spiral machine. We should someone should show us how. I don't know do you? I can make the holes but the spiral in it. i hate it.

Silhouettes of Simon Giving Oral to Things

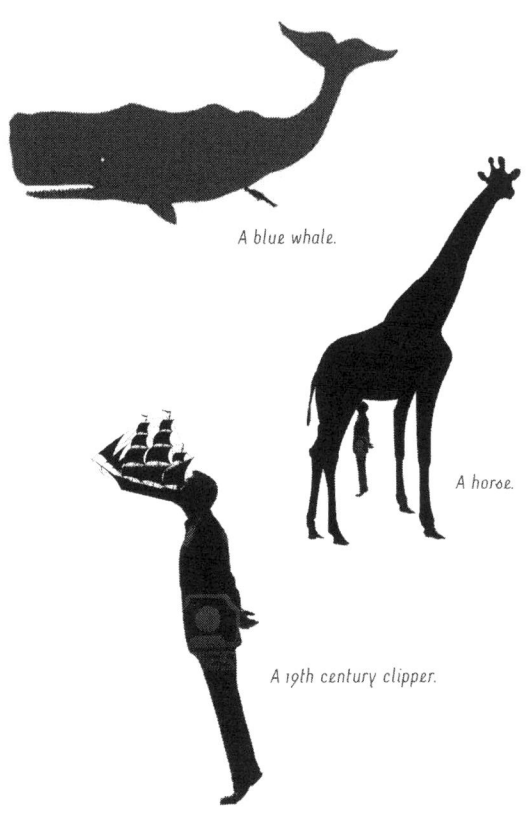

A blue whale.

A horse.

A 19th century clipper.

Ten Formal Complaints

I don't really have anything against Simon apart from the fact that he likes the band Nickelback and I have no idea what his problem with me is as I'm a pleasure to work with. I brought in donuts once. I found them in a bin and left them near Simon's desk. When he asked, "Who brought these donuts in?" I replied, "The girl from the shop across the road. They had too many" and watched him eat four, complaining between mouthfuls that they weren't very fresh. He would have eaten them all but stopped after finding a dead cricket in the box.

My first run in with Simon was when he blamed me for stealing pens from his desk, which I vehemently denied. He then proceeded to point out the tiny engraved words 'Simon's Pen' he had done on all eight of the pens currently on my desk. Each two-millimetre letter was meticulous. When I asked how he had managed to get the letters so perfect, he told me that he had a headset at home with a light and magnifying glass on it. When I asked why he had a headset with light and magnifying glass on it he replied, "For painting collector figurines."

There have actually been twelve formal complaints by Simon against me but two of those were complaining that nothing had been done about the previous formal complaints so I didn't bother scanning those in.

F26-A

Date JUN 13 /2011   **Date of offense** JUNE 13 2011

Name of person filing F26-A SIMON DEMPSEY

Name/s of person/s involved DAVID THORNE

Complaint type [✓] Internal [ ] External [ ] Other:

Description   Ref: [✓] Formal [ ] Med [ ] Class 1 [ ] Class 2

WHILE I WAS AT LUNCH A PACKAGE CAME FOR ME BECAUSE I ORDERED A TSHIRT ONLINE LAST WEEK. IT WAS ON MY DESK AND WHEN I OPENED IT THERE WAS A PAIR OF SOCKS IN IT AND I COULD TELL THE PACKAGE HAD BEEN OPENED AND TAPED BACK UP. WHEN I WENT INTO DAVID THORNES OFFICE HE WAS WEARING THE TSHIRT. HE DID NOT HAVE MY PERMISSION TO OPEN THE PACKAGE OR TOUCH MY PERSONAL PROPERTY

Action Requested [✓] Disciplinary [ ] Mediation [ ] Other:

Signature _(signed)_   JUN/13 /2011

Office Use Only

RECEIVED

Ref [X] F26-A [ ] F26-B   Lodged: [X] Y [ ] N

F26-B Attached [ ] Y [X] N   Date JUN 13 2011

F26-A

Date JUNE 7/2011 | **Date of offence** JUNE 7 2011

Name of person filing F26-A SIMON DEMPSEY

Name/s of person/s involved DAVID THORNE

Complaint type ☑ Internal ☐ External ☐ Other:

Description Ref: ☑ Formal ☐ Med ☑ Class 1 ☐ Class 2

WHILE I WAS IN A MEETING THIS MORNING, DAVID THORNE REPLACED MY OFFICE CHAIR WITH AN EXERCISE BIKE. I DON'T KNOW WHAT HE HAS DONE WITH MY CHAIR AND I DON'T KNOW WHERE HE GOT THE EXERCISE BIKE. THIS IS A WASTE OF COMPANY TIME AND RESOURCES.

Action Requested ☑ Disciplinary ☐ Mediation ☑ Other: RETURN IT

Signature JUNE 17/2011

Office Use Only

Ref ☒ F26-A ☐ F26-B | Lodged: ☒ Y ☐ N RECEIVED

F26-B Attached ☐ Y ☒ N | Date JUN 7 2011

F26-A

Date JUL/12/2011　　**Date of offense** July 7 2011

Name of person filing F26-A　SIMON DEMPSEY

Name/s of person/s involved　DAVID THORNE

Complaint type　[✓] Internal　[ ] External　[ ] Other:

Description　　Ref: [✓] Formal　[ ] Med　[ ] Class 1　[ ] Class 2

DAVID THORNE KEEPS ANSWERING THE PHONE BY SAYING HELLO THIS IS SIMON DEMPSEY. I HAVE ASKED HIM TO STOP BUT HE IS STILL DOING IT. SCOTT FROM APB RANG AND ASKED FOR A PDF AND DAVID SAID HE COULDNT DO IT RIGHT AWAY BECAUSE IT IS TIME FOR HIS NAP. THIS IS UNPROFFESIONAL AND MAKES ME LOOK BAD TO THE CLIENT. HE ALSO KEEPS SENDING ME VIDEOS USING PHOTOBOOTH TO MAKE IT LOOK LIKE HE IS ON A ROLLER COASTER. THIS IS WASTING COMPANY TIME AND INTERNET.

Action Requested　[✓] Disciplinary　[ ] Mediation　[ ] Other:

Signature　　　　　　　　　　　　　　　　JUL/12/2011

Office Use Only

Ref　[X] F26-A　[ ] F26-B　　**Lodged:** [X] Y　[ ] N　　RECEIVED

F26-B Attached　[ ] Y　[X] N　　**Date** JUL 12 2011

F26-A

Date JUL 15 /2011   **Date of offense** JULY 15 2011

Name of person filing F26-A SIMON DEMPSEY

Name/s of person/s involved DAVID THORNE

Complaint type [✓] Internal [ ] External [ ] Other:

Description   Ref: [✓] Formal [ ] Med [ ] Class 1 [ ] Class 2

I PUT A TUPPERWARE CONTAINER IN THE FRIDGE THAT HAD A SANDWICH AND A KITKAT IN IT AND WHEN I OPENED IT AT LUNCH TIME THERE WAS A PICKLE IN IT INSTEAD. THIS IS STEALING. I KNOW IT WAS DAVID THORNE BECAUSE HE SAID I SHOULD GO TO LUNCH EARLY BECAUSE I DESERVE A BREAK TODAY WHICH IS WHAT THEY SAY IN THE KITKAT ADVERT. HE DID NOT HAVE PERMISSION TO TAKE MY PROPERTY.

Action Requested [✓] Disciplinary [ ] Mediation [ ] Other:

Signature   JUL /15 /2011

Office Use Only

Ref [X] F26-A [ ] F26-B   **Lodged:** [ ] Y [X] N   RECEIVED

F26-B Attached [ ] Y [X] N   **Date** JUL 15 2011

F26-A

Date AUG 11 / 2011 **Date of offense** AUG 11 2011

Name of person filing F26-A SIMON DEMPSEY

Name/s of person/s involved DAVID THORNE

Complaint type [✓] Internal [ ] External [ ] Other:

Description Ref: [✓] Formal [ ] Med [ ] Class 1 [ ] Class 2

I HAD 2 BOXES OF BUSINESS CARDS IN MY DESK DRAWER AND SOMETIME IN THE LAST MONTH DAVID THORNE REPLACED THEM WITH CARDS THAT HAVE MY TITLE CHANGED FROM GRAPHIC DESIGNER TO HORSE WHISPERER. I DONT KNOW WHEN HE CHANGED THEM SO I DONT KNOW HOW MANY I HAVE GIVEN OUT TO PEOPLE. THIS IS A WASTE OF COMPANY MONEY AND UNPROFESSIONAL.

Action Requested [✓] Disciplinary [ ] Mediation [ ] Other:

Signature *(signed)*   AUG / 11 / 2011

Office Use Only

Ref [✗] F26-A [ ] F26-B   Lodged: [✗] Y [ ] N

F26-B Attached [ ] Y [✗] N   Date AUG 11, 2011 / 2011

RECEIVED

F26-A

Date MAR/25/2011 **Date of offense** MARCH 25 2011

Name of person filing F26-A SIMON DEMPSEY

Name/s of person/s involved DAVID THORNE

Complaint type [✓] Internal [✓] External [ ] Other:

Description Ref: [✓] Formal [ ] Med [ ] Class 1 [ ] Class 2

SOMETIME EITHER THIS MORNING OR LAST NIGHT DAVID THORNE GLUED PICTURES OF HIS FACE ONTO THE NICKELBACK POSTER ABOVE MY DESK. HE USED SPRAY ADHESIVE AND WHEN I TRIED TO PEEL THEM OFF IT RIPPED THE PAPER. THIS IS DAMAGING MY PERSONAL PROPERTY. HE MUST HAVE SPRAYED ON MY DESK BECAUSE THERE IS A FILM OF ADHESIVE ALL OVER MY DESK AND MY ARMS STICK TO IT WHEN I AM USING MY COMPUTER.

Action Requested [✓] Disciplinary [ ] Mediation [ ] Other:

Signature   MAR/25/2011

Office Use Only

RECEIVED

Ref [X] F26-A [ ] F26-B   **Lodged:** [X] Y [ ] N

F26-B Attached [ ] Y [X] N   **Date** MAR 25 2011/2011

From: Simon Dempsey
Date: Thursday 31 March 2011 12.37pm
To: David Thorne
Subject: No Subject

Did you draw Justin Biebers face on all the images in my stock images folder and save them over my files?

....

From: David Thorne
Date: Thursday 31 March 2011 12.44pm
To: Simon Dempsey
Subject: Re: No Subject

Yes.

....

From: Simon Dempsey
Date: Thursday 31 March 2011 12.49pm
To: David Thorne
Subject: Re: Re: No Subject

What the fuck for? What are you even doing in my files?

....

From: David Thorne
Date: Thursday 31 March 2011 12.56pm
To: Simon Dempsey
Subject: Re: Re: Re: No Subject

I didn't think you'd notice. I'm meant to be laying out a

business card for a client so was looking for a distraction and realised I can open and save files from your computer over the network.

From: Simon Dempsey
Date: Thursday 31 March 2011 1.05pm
To: David Thorne
Subject: Re: Re: Re: Re: No Subject

But why did you put Justin Biebers face on them dickwad? I was going to use them for something.

From: David Thorne
Date: Thursday 31 March 2011 1.12pm
To: Simon Dempsey
Subject: Re: Re: Re: Re: Re: No Subject

You still can. Justin Bieber is very popular.

From: Simon Dempsey
Date: Thursday 31 March 2011 1.43pm
To: David Thorne
Subject: Re: Re: Re: Re: Re: Re: Re: No Subject

Right dickhead. I'm making a formal complaint.

F26-A

Date APRIL 4 / 2011   **Date of offense** APRIL 4, 2011

Name of person filing F26-A   SIMON DEMPSEY

Name/s of person/s involved   DAVID THORNE

Complaint type [✓] Internal [ ] External [ ] Other:

Description   Ref: [✓] Formal [ ] Med [ ] Class 1 [ ] Class 2

WHILE I WAS AT LUNCH DAVID THORNE WENT ON MY COMPUTER OR WENT ON IT OVER THE NETWORK WITHOUT MY PERMISSION AND HE PHOTOSHOPPED JUSTIN BIEBERS FACE ONTO ALL THE PHOTOS IN MY PERSONAL STOCK IMAGES FOLDER. HE DID NOT HAVE MY PERMISSION AND HE ADMITTED TO DOING IT. THIS IS A WASTE OF COMPANY TIME AND DAMAGE TO MY PERSONAL PROPERTY.

Action Requested [✓] Disciplinary [ ] Mediation [ ] Other:

Signature   APRIL 4 / 2011

Office Use Only

RECEIVED

Ref [X] F26-A [ ] F26-B   **Lodged:** [X] Y [ ] N

F26-B Attached [ ] Y [X] N   **Date** APR 04 2011

F26-A

Date MAY/ 11 /2011   Date of offense MAY /1 2011

Name of person filing F26-A SIMON DEMPSEY

Name/s of person/s involved DAVID THORNE

Complaint type [✓] Internal [ ] External [ ] Other:

Description   Ref: [✓] Formal [ ] Med [ ] Class 1 [ ] Class 2

WHILE I WAS DOWNSTAIRS IN THE WIP MEETING, DAVID THORNE PAINTED MY IPHONE WHITE WITH LIQUID PAPER. THIS IS DAMAGING MY PERSONAL PROPERTY. IT IS THE 3RD TIME HE HAS DAMAGED MY PROPERTY ON PURPOSE. I KNOW IT WAS HIM BECAUSE BEFORE I WENT INTO THE MEETING I SAID I WANTED THE NEW WHITE IPHONE. THERE IS LIQUID PAPER IN THE PLUG THAT THE HEADPHONES GO INTO.

Action Requested [✓] Disciplinary [ ] Mediation [✓] Other: REPLACE IT

Signature   MAY /11 /2011

Office Use Only

RECEIVED

Ref [✓] F26-A [ ] F26-B   Lodged: [✓] Y [ ] N

F26-B Attached [ ] Y [✓] N   Date MAY 12 20)1 2011

F26-A

Date MAR 19 /2011 **Date of offense** MARCH 9 2011

Name of person filing F26-A SIMON DEMPSEY

Name/s of person/s involved DAVID THORNE

Complaint type [✓] Internal [ ] External [ ] Other:

Description Ref: [✓] Formal [ ] Med [ ] Class 1 [ ] Class 2

WHILE I WAS AWAY YESTERDAY DAVID THORNE MOVED MY DESK INTO THE KITCHEN AND MOVED THE WATER COOLER AND BOOKSHELF AND THE BIG PLANT TO WHERE MY DESK WAS AND HE CHANGED THE PHOTO OF KAREN I HAD IN THE FRAME TO A PHOTO OF THE FRIDGE. THIS IS TAKING PERSONAL PROPERTY AND WASTING COMPANY TIME BECAUSE IT TOOK ME 2 HOURS TO MOVE IT ALL BACK BY MYSELF BECAUSE HE SAID HE WAS TOO BUSY RESEARCHING WASPS TO HELP.

Action Requested [✓] Disciplinary [ ] Mediation [ ] Other:

Signature MARCH 19 /2011

Office Use Only

Ref [✗] F26-A [ ] F26-B **Lodged:** [✗] Y [ ] N

F26-B Attached [ ] Y [✗] N **Date** /MAR 09 2011

RECEIVED

F26-A

| Date | 15 / AUG / 2011 | Date of offence | 15 AUG 2011 |

Name of person filing F26-A: SIMON DEMPSEY

Name/s of person/s involved: DAVID THORNE

Complaint type: ☑ Internal ☐ External ☐ Other:

Description   Ref: ☑ Formal ☐ Med ☑ Class 1 ☐ Class 2

DAVID THORNE CHANGED MY PROFILE TEXT ON THE WEBSITE TO STUFF ABOUT ME WANTING TO MARRY MY MOM AND OTHER STUFF. I DONT NOT KNOW WHEN HE CHANGED IT SO LOTS OF PEOPLE COULD HAVE READ IT. THIS IS A WASTE OF COMPANY TIME AND RESOURCES AND IS UNPROFESSIONAL.

Action Requested: ☑ Disciplinary ☐ Mediation ☐ Other:

Signature: [signature]   15 AUG / 2011

Office Use Only

RECEIVED

Ref: ☑ F26-A ☐ F26-B   Lodged: ☑ Y ☐ N

F26-B Attached: ☐ Y ☑ N   Date AUG/15/2011

Home | strategic branding | **our people** | associates | client login | contact us

Our People / Simon Dempsey

Simon has worked here since 1904 as a potted plant. Popular with the ladies, Simon enjoys knitting leg-warmers for his cats and performing dance extravaganzas for his mother. He is the founding and sole member of *The Dempsey Dance Academy* and meets once a week to discuss late membership fees. His best friend is a dead bee he found on his windowsill in 2004 which he named Simon.

Simon speaks fluent Simonese, a language he developed using only vowels. He is adept at sewing and owns a Singer Stylist 7258. By using a magnifying glass, Simon has created over three-hundred costumes for his bee ranging from jogging outfits to red carpet attire.

Simon's key specialty is wearing shirts the same colour as the walls. He is also an expert at sitting very still and has held a variety of positions including stretched out, standing on tippy-toes with his hands on his hips, and crouched. Once, when Simon was young, he saw a horse. Simon has a tattoo on his lower back of musician Kenny Rogers and has an extensive working knowledge of the latest technologies including metric. His favourite music is his own which he creates on his RCA cassette recorder by humming and clapping. Each Friday night, for the last four years, he has invited his neighbours over to listen. Attendance has been disappointing despite the offer of free cabbage.

Simon is currently single but one day hopes to marry his mother because of her "good child-bearing hips." In the meantime, Simon is active on several dating sites under the username *Mr Bobbity*. His last online girlfriend, who he dated off and on for three years, turned out to be an auto-responder. On weekends, Simon enjoys thermostat regulation, making lists of things that are blue, collecting felt, and trampolining. His career goal is to one day establish a floating city in the Pacific Ocean where he will be king and everyone will have to do what he says.

F26-A

Date Feb / 17 / 2011   **Date of offense** FEB 17 2011

Name of person filing F26-A   SIMON DEMPSEY

Name/s of person/s involved   DAVID THORNE

Complaint type [✓] Internal [ ] External [ ] Other:

Description   Ref: [✓] Formal [ ] Med [ ] Class 1 [ ] Class 2

DAVID THORNE CHANGED MY HOME PAGE SO INSTEAD OF GOOGLE IT GOES TO A MAN SINGING. I DID NOT GIVE HIM PERMISSION TO GO ON MY COMPUTER. I HAVE CHANGED IT BACK BUT IT KEEPS HAPPENING. HE ALSO CHANGED THE P AND W KEYS AROUND ON MY KEYBOARD SO IT OPENS THE PRINT BOX INSTEAD OF CLOSING THE WINDOW AND THE PLASTIC BIT BROKE OFF WHEN I TRIED TO CHANGE THEM BACK. THIS IS DAMAGING COMPANY PROPERTY.

Action Requested [✓] Disciplinary [ ] Mediation [ ] Other:

Signature   FEB / 17 / 2011

Office Use Only

Ref [✗] F26-A [ ] F26-B   Lodged: [✗] Y [ ] N   RECEIVED
F26-B Attached [ ] Y [✗] N   Date FEB 17 2011

F26-A

Date: APRIL 6 / 2011   Date of offense: APRIL 6 2011

Name of person filing F26-A: SIMON DEMPSEY

Name/s of person/s involved: DAVID THORNE

Complaint type: [✓] Internal [ ] External [ ] Other:

Description   Ref: [✓] Formal [ ] Med [ ] Class 1 [ ] Class 2

I GOT AN EMAIL FROM LOUISE SAYING THAT I HAD TO PAY $75 FOR SWIMMING LESSONS BECAUSE IT IS COMPANY SAFETY REGULATION. WHEN I GAVE HER THE MONEY SHE DIDN'T KNOW ANYTHING ABOUT IT. I KNOW IT WAS DAVID THORNE BECAUSE WHEN I ASKED HIM IF HE HAD TO DO THE LESSONS AS WELL HE SAID NO BECAUSE HE SHOWED LOUISE A COPY OF HIS HIGH SCHOOL SWIMMING CERTIFICATE. BUT THERE ARE NO LESSONS. YOU CAN'T SEND EMAILS FROM OTHER PEOPLE. THIS IS FRAUD AND A WASTE OF COMPANY TIME.

Action Requested: [✓] Disciplinary [ ] Mediation [ ] Other:

Signature: [signed]   APRI 6 / 2011

Office Use Only

Ref: [✓] F26-A [ ] F26-B   Lodged: [✓] Y [ ] N   RECEIVED
F26-B Attached: [ ] Y [✓] N   Date: APR 06 2011

F26-A

Date 10 /AUG/ 2011 | **Date of offense** 10 AUG 2011

Name of person filing F26-A SIMON DEMPSEY

Name/s of person/s involved DAVID THORNE

Complaint type [✓] Internal [ ] External [ ] Other:

Description Ref: [✓] Formal [ ] Med [✓] Class 1 [ ] Class 2

I TOOK MY CAR TO A MECHANIC TODAY BECAUSE IT WAS MAKING A NOISE WHEN I DROVE IT AND THE MECHANIC FOUND A HORN STUCK IN THE GRILL WITH PLAYDOH, HIDDEN. I KNOW IT WAS DAVID BECAUSE WHO ELSE WOULD DO IT?

Action Requested [✓] Disciplinary [ ] Mediation [ ] Other:

Signature _[signature]_ 10 AUG/ 2011

Office Use Only

Ref [✓] F26-A [ ] F26-B | Lodged: [✓] Y [ ] N

F26-B Attached [ ] Y [✓] N | Date AUG 10 2011

RECEIVED

ATT: David Thorne
RE: Employee Formal Notice
DATE: Oct 31 2012

Dear David,

This correspondence is to notify you that a complaint made against you on Oct 19 2012 by Simon Dempsey has been discussed in a meeting of department heads who agree a formal notice is warranted. This notice covers additional complaints filed by Simon on September 12 and 14 and October 9 and 16.

We appreciate the creative department has its own way of doing things that are rarely in line with company procedures and as such you are given a lot of leeway. Unfortunately, in this instance Simon has filed an F-26B with his complaint so we are obligated to act on his complaints as per head office policy.

Please accept this as a first formal notice and address the following to ensure further action is not warranted:

1. At no time are you permitted to change the thermostat setting in Simon's office.

2. At no time are you permitted to pretend to be Simon Dempsey while answering the telephone. This includes both internal and outside calls. If Simon is absent from his desk, you are also not to answer his phone by making cat noises. All calls are to be answered in a professional manner. In addition, at no time are you permitted to send or reply to emails under Simon's name or order items using Simon's online accounts. You will pay all return shipping fees for the 36 boxes of Kleenex and vibrating seat cushion.

3. At no time are you permitted to dance in Simon's office. Please be mindful of the needs of others to work without interruption or distraction. This includes dancing past Simon's door, dancing in your office when he can see you from his desk, and sending Simon videos of you dancing. While there is no company policy against dancing, it would be preferred that this activity was kept to break areas away from others and during company functions where appropriate. In addition, at no time are you permitted to call Simon's mobile phone from your office and hang up just as he answers it. Due to the frequency of this occurring, it is clearly not the case that you forgot what you were calling him for.

4. At no time are you permitted to glue anything to, on, or near Simon's desk. This includes both company and personal items. Spray adhesive is to be used only in the spray booth with the vacuum activated, not near Simon's desk or monitor. The ceramic giraffe and sea shells that are permanently attached to Simon's desk with super-glue are to be removed.

5. At no time is Simon to be referred to by any name but his own. All references to Bob the Badger, Mr Bobbity Head and Señor Bob, including those on the company website, are to be changed back. In addition, at no time are you permitted to take photos of Simon without his permission. All photos of Simon on the wall of your office with pieces of string leading to photos of murder victims are to be removed and the photo on the company website of Simon eating a hotdog is to be replaced with Simon's original staff photograph.

Sincerely

Jennifer Haines
Human Resources Manager

Timesheets

I'm not a fan of doing timesheets. I mentioned this to my partner Holly and she said, "God you are lazy, just write down when you arrive and leave. How hard can it be?" Which must apparently be how it works in non-design related companies.

Although designers are rarely known for their organisational skills, we're expected to compile a methodical record throughout the day of each project we are working on. I refuse to do this partly because there are far too many unaccountable hours to explain and partly because if I wanted to 'clock in, clock off,' I'd work in a factory. Making garage-door remotes or something. Even then, I doubt I would be expected to write down 'Made a garage-door remote' after making each garage-door remote.

I'm not a fan of most office procedures actually. I did once implement my own where, at 4.30pm each day, everyone would insult each other for fifteen minutes and then, for the last fifteen minutes of each day, apologise to each person for what had been said. This way, everyone would leave happy with all issues sorted. It didn't go as well as expected. Two formal complaints were made and the secretary locked herself in the toilet and cried.

Also, I received a bit of flack after posting a series of formal complaints recently. Apparently, I was picking on Simon for no other reason than to be cruel. While that may be true, there are many other reasons to pick on Simon. Here are just three:

1. Simon super-glued his calculator to his desk to stop people borrowing it. Its position at the back of the desk and the angle of the LCD screen requires that he stand to use it.

2. Simon times and records toilet breaks and personal calls on his timesheets. He also times and records the time it takes him to do his timesheets on his timesheets.

3. I once asked Simon what three items he would rescue from a house fire and he replied, "My cat, the home insurance policy, and my Invicta watch collection."

From: Simon Dempsey
Date: Monday 13 February 2012 9.11am
To: David Thorne
Subject: Timesheets

Did you use my desk while I was away?

You're not allowed to go on my computer. I can tell someone used it because I shut it down before I left and pulled out the power cord but it was on this morning and where is my mousepad and what is this shit drawn on my desk?

I need to collect everyones time sheets for last week as well. Have you done them?

From: David Thorne
Date: Monday 13 February 2012 9.52am
To: Simon Dempsey
Subject: Re: Timesheets

Good morning Simon,

No, I have decided not to do timesheets anymore. I'm not a robot. As your new token responsibility as time-sheet collector is essentially the office equivalent of placing an OCD child in charge of equally spaced fridge-magnet distribution to keep it occupied while *The View* is on, this saves you from having to bother with the whole embarrassing process.

Also, while I generally avoid going anywhere near your cubicle of sorrow - in case the lack of atmosphere causes my eyes to pop out like in that Arnold Schwarzenegger movie where he is on Mars and his eyes pop out - I was required to access your computer in your absence due to a client's request for files.

I actually missed you while you were away. To counter this, I placed a plank of wood in your chair and wrote 'Simon' on it. He said I could use your stuff.

Regards, David.

Attached image: Foyer.jpg

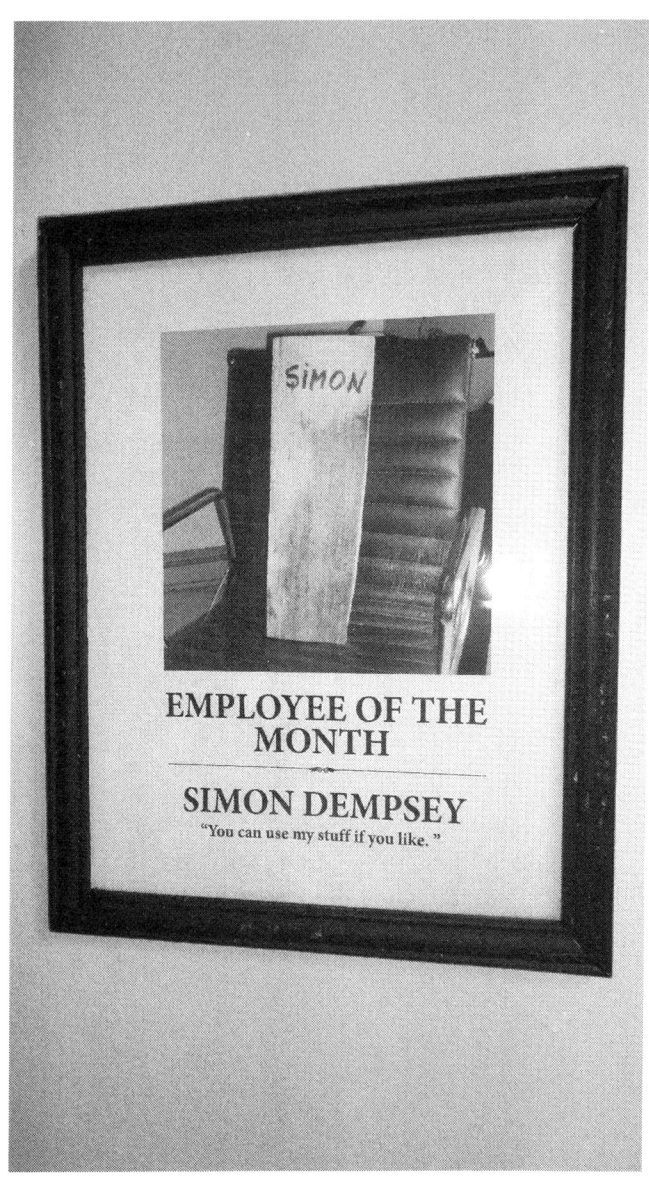

From: Simon Dempsey
Date: Monday 13 February 2012 10.05am
To: David Thorne
Subject: Re: Re: Timesheets

YOURE NOT ALLOWED TO USE MY COMPUTER.

What client needed a file off my computer? Youre not allowed to put things on the walls in the foyer either. It leaves holes. It was a waste of time anyway because I took it straight down. Some of us have work to do you know.

And you don't just get to choose if you do your timesheets or not. You're not special. Its the rules and accounts need them to bill the client properly. I've been here longer than you and I put my time sheets in every week. Everyone has to do them.

1. YOURE NOT ALLOWED NOT TOUCH MY COMPUTER

2. DO NOT USE MY STUFF

3. YOU HAVE TO DO YOUR TIMESHEETS. EVERYONE DOES.

I took a photo of my desk and I'm going to email it to Jennifer. Is it permanent marker?

And where are my pens dickhead?

From: David Thorne
Date: Monday 13 February 2012 11.08am
To: Simon Dempsey
Subject: Re: Re: Re: Timesheets

Dear Simon,

As you are aware, all branding services provided by this company are charged at a fixed quote and price. As such, time spent doing timesheets might be better spent questioning the logic of requiring timesheets to calculate a fee that has already been agreed upon.

Or cleaning your desk.

I read about five monkeys once that were placed in a room with a banana at the top of a set of stairs. As one monkey attempted to climb the stairs, all of the monkeys were sprayed with jets of cold water. A second monkey made an attempt and again the monkeys were sprayed. No more monkeys attempted to climb the stairs. One of the monkeys was then removed from the room and replaced with a new monkey. The new monkey saw the banana and started to climb the stairs but, to its surprise, it was attacked by the other monkeys. Another of the original monkeys was replaced and the newcomer was also attacked when he attempted to climb the stairs.

The previous newcomer took part in the punishment with enthusiasm.

A third replacement monkey headed for the stairs and was attacked as well. Half of the monkeys that attacked him had no idea why. After replacing the fourth and fifth original monkeys, none had ever been sprayed with cold water but every single one of them stayed the fuck away from the stairs.

Being here longer than me doesn't automatically make your adherence to a rule, or the rule itself, right. It makes you the fifth replacement monkey. The one with the weird red arse and the first to point and screech when anyone approaches the stairs. I would be the sixth monkey, at home in bed trying to come up with a viable excuse not to spend another fruitless day locked in a room with five neurotic monkeys.

Regardless, you will be pleased to learn that due to your absence last week leaving me with a spare hour per day, which is usually dedicated to staring at the back of your head with one eye closed doing that thing with your thumb and finger where you squash it, I did do my timesheets.

Please find attached.

Regards, David.

MONDAY

9am
Arrived at work. Considered staying home in bed but, with Simon being away this week, there's no real reason to be absent. Checked production schedule. Completed my work for the week.

4pm
Cleaned my mouse.

5pm
Left for the day.

TUESDAY

10am
Arrived at work. Answered the phone on Simon's desk with "Hello, this is Simon Dempsey speaking. How may I be of help to you?" Told client I would have a pdf to them "as quick as a cheetah."

10.30am
Accessed Simon's computer using his secret password 'Archmage' in order to locate and send requested pdf to client. Sent.

Read Simon's emails. Replied to his mother regarding her question about what to get Auntie Maureen for her birthday. Recommended jumping castle.

11.30am
Attempted to log into Simon's Facebook. Clicked 'send me my password.' Checked Simon's email. Logged into Simon's Facebook. Changed status to single.

Sent Karen a message saying "Ignore the status change. We haven't broken up. I just don't want anyone to know I have a girlfriend."

Looked at pictures Simon uploaded of himself in a boat. Googled the names of the two guys in *Miami Vice*. Tagged Simon's nipples 'Sony' and 'Chubbs'.

4pm
Left for the day.

WEDNESDAY

11.am
Arrived at work. Read about Emperor Penguins on Wikipedia while having my morning coffee at Simon's desk. Drew pictures of penguins.

11.30am
Realised the permanent Sharpie I was drawing with had penetrated the paper and Simon's desk now had eighteen penguins saying 'Hey' on it.

Hunting for something to clean it with, I used the key Simon hides behind the framed photo of his cat Lady Diana to unlock his top drawer. Found Star Wars Lego.

Recreated the scene from the movie where, during a lightsaber duel, Vader cuts off Luke's right hand, reveals that he is his father, and entreats him to convert to the dark side so they can rule the galaxy as father and son. Lost Luke's hand behind Simon's desk.

12.30pm
Chased and killed a bee in the office with Simon's mousepad rolled into a tube while making lightsaber noises. Closed Simon's window.

12.45pm
Thought about the bee's family waiting expectantly at home for his return. Gave them names. Imagined Bradley rushing into his mother's outstretched arms, bewailing, "I miss him so much" and Brenda replying, "I know Bradley, I miss him too."

Performed ceremony. There was cake. Constructed a small funereal pyre on Simon's desk out of a paperclip, placed Ben's small lifeless body on top, mentioned his selfless determination to provide for his family, and set it alight.

I was only into the first verse of Bohemian Rhapsody, the only church song I know, when Ben's body popped like a corn kernel and flew behind the desk. Unsure if he was still alight, I poured coffee down after him.

Realising nobody has ever been behind Simon's desk due to its size and position against a rear wall, I also dropped the remains of the cake and the plate down the back to save me having to walk into the kitchen.

Accidently knocked Simon's pens down there as well. And then his mousepad.

3pm
Left for the day.

THURSDAY

12pm
Arrived at work. Sat in Simon's chair without my pants on.

2pm
Left for the day.

FRIDAY

Called in sick. Went shopping. Bought a Keurig.

....

From: Simon Dempsey
Date: Monday 13 February 2012 11.29am
To: David Thorne
Subject: Re: Re: Re: Re: Timesheets

Thanks for the evidence dickhead. I forwarded that to Jennifer and i changed my password. I'm making a formal complaint. Stay off my computer or I will punch you in the throat. I'm serious. Are you going to get my stuff out from behind the desk?

From: David Thorne
Date: Monday 13 February 2012 11.41am
To: Simon Dempsey
Subject: Re: Re: Re: Re: Re: Timesheets

Dear Simon,

I wish I had the time. Some of us have work to do and timesheets to complete. I have attached today's should you wish to also email them to Jennifer.

Regards, David

MONDAY

9am
Arrived at work. I feel it is important to set a good example for the other staff through promptness.

9.11am
Received a series of rather vicious emails from Simon, which began with accusations, insults, questions and demands, and degraded into actual threats of bodily harm. This was after I told him I had missed him while he was away. I find this unprovoked animosity disappointing and would have expected more from the employee of the month.

11.30am
Filled out these time sheets as it is part of the job and allows production to bill the client accordingly. Finding it difficult to concentrate on job priorities today due to the negative

environment Simon has created, will therefore be leaving at lunch time.

....

From: Simon Dempsey
Date: Monday 13 February 2012 11.53am
To: David Thorne
Subject: Re: Re: Re: Re: Re: Re: Timesheets

Good. I wont have to see your ugly head if you go early. Youre the one who will get in trouble dickhead.

....

From: David Thorne
Date: Monday 13 February 2012 12.09pm
To: Simon Dempsey
Subject: Re: Re: Re: Re: Re: Re: Re: Timesheets

Attached image: Foyer2.jpg

Team Building

Whoever came up with the phrase, "Hell is other people" probably worked in a design agency... I just googled it, apparently it was a French guy with a girl's name who never worked in a design agency. If Jean-Paul Sartre had worked in our design agency, he wouldn't have lasted a week. Mainly because he doesn't have a background in design.

I'm not a huge fan of time spent with co-workers. Mainly because it usually means being at work and I am a huge fan of not being at work. When I do attend, I spend the whole day coming up with an excuse not to be there the next day so really it's time that would be better spent on a hobby or something.

Occasionally, I'm expected to spend time with co-workers outside of office hours. Last year, it was three days on a houseboat stuck on a sandbar. The year before that, Mike organised a camping trip to a lake he had visited when he was a child. After purchasing kayaks and tents, renting a trailer, and driving for eight hours, we arrived to find the town abandoned due to the lake drying up several years prior so we drove back. I did get to poke a lizard with a stick though, so it wasn't a complete waste of time.

From: Mike Campbell
Date: Monday 14 March 2011 9.06am
To: All Staff
Subject: Staff weekend

Kevin and I had a meeting last week to discuss doing a staff team-building weekend. It's tax deductible and we can get a package deal with a place on the river that looks nice. It has activities like yoga, canoeing, hiking, orienteering and a talent night.

It's a 2 hour drive so if we leave Friday after lunch, we'll get there before 4pm allowing for stops along the way. The plan is to lock in the 25th to the 27th of this month so can everyone check their schedules and confirm these dates with Melissa please?

Mike

From: David Thorne
Date: Monday 14 March 2011 9.34am
To: Mike Campbell
Subject: Re: Staff weekend

Mike,

How is driving two hours to participate in group activities that involve being sweaty, judged and lost with people we dislike, any different to a normal day here ?

David

From: Mike Campbell
Date: Monday 14 March 2011 10.04am
To: David Thorne
Subject: Re: Re: Staff weekend

I should have known you'd be the first to complain. Everyone else had a good time last year on the houseboat.

Mike

....

From: David Thorne
Date: Monday 14 March 2011 11.22am
To: Mike Campbell
Subject: Re: Re: Re: Staff weekend

Mike,

It was a question, not a complaint. I'm the last to complain about anything. If I were on a game show where points were awarded for complaining, my only complaint would be participating in a show that is clearly beyond my means of winning. At the end of the show, I would thank the host for having me and say I had a wonderful time anyway.

My favorite part of the houseboat was when we were stuck on a sandbar for three days. Unable to radio for help, due to your hair-dryer draining the batteries, you claimed yourself captain and ordered me to swim ashore and climb a tree to get phone reception. It's not mutiny if the captain can't provide sufficient evidence to support his title and you refused to accept my title of *Grand Admiral Emperor King of Everything* the next day.

My second favourite part of the trip was when you drank three day's alcohol supply on the first afternoon, fell from the bow, and yelled at me for not diving in to rescue you. In my defense, I felt the best thing would be being able to later provide an accurate eyewitness account. I would have left out the bit where you screamed, "Something touched my leg! Not like this. Not like this."

Just this morning, while feigning interest in Jodie's dilemma regarding missing Farmville credits and watching Simon pick his nose and wipe it under his desk, I thought to myself, "The one thing missing in my life is a greater percentage of time spent with these people."

If I take a compass with me on the hike does that mean I can skip orienteering? This would leave me with only yoga, canoeing and talent night to avoid participating in.

David

From: Mike Campbell
Date: Monday 14 March 2011 11.46am
To: David Thorne
Subject: Re: Re: Re: Re: Staff weekend

It wasn't 3 days, it was less than 24 hours. And what's the point of going if you're not going to participate in TEAM activities??

Mike

From: David Thorne
Date: Monday 14 March 2011 1.09pm
To: Mike Campbell
Subject: Re: Re: Re: Re: Re: Staff weekend

Mike,

My point exactly. It might be interesting to see what talents the staff comes up with for talent night though. I've been here for a year and haven't seen any.

Yoga is definitely out of the question - witnessing Kevin and Simon clad in Spandex, rolling around on the floor like a couple of neon walruses engaged in a territorial dispute, is probably a breach of OH&S regulations.

I'm fine with kayaking though. As long as I can sit in the back and pretend to paddle only when the person in the front turns around to complain about me not paddling. It might be a nice break from avoiding activities. If it's one of those little single-person kayaks, my non-paddling will have the added benefit of failing to keep up with the group - as you all pass a bend in the river, I'll have the opportunity, should I decide to take it, to roll the kayak and drown.

Also, what are the sleeping arrangements? I won't share with Simon again after our last business trip. I was unable to sleep due to his controlled breathing and rustling. It was around 1am before I realised why he had placed the mini hair-conditioner bottle from the hotel bathroom on his side table and what the squeezing and slapping noises were.

I've attached a diagram indicating proposed travel, sleeping and activity arrangements.

I'm A, everyone else is B, and C is a lockable door.

David.

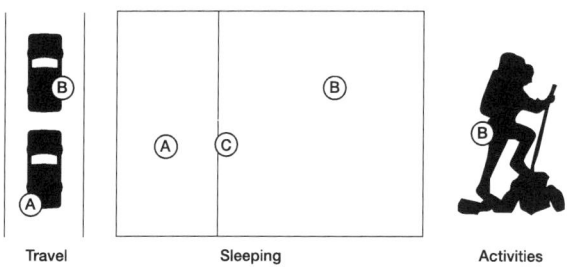

| Travel | Sleeping | Activities |

From: Mike Campbell
Date: Monday 14 March 2011 1.18pm
To: David Thorne
Subject: Re: Re: Re: Re: Re: Re: Staff weekend

You're going. And you will participate in the activities because we've already booked and paid. You're in a shared double with Ben. You're not getting your own room because the lodge already cost us nearly $5000 and Melissa's budgeted another $1000 for alcohol at the bar.

From: Melissa Peters
Date: Monday 14 March 2011 2.26pm
To: David Thorne
Subject: Hey

Hi, are you attending the staff weekend on the 25th? I need to confirm final numbers.

Mel

....

From: David Thorne
Date: Monday 14 March 2011 2.41pm
To: Melissa Peters
Subject: Re: Hey

Looking forward to it.

Also, Mike asked that you change my room to a single because Ben has scabies.

David

....

From: Melissa Peters
Date: Monday 14 March 2011 2.57pm
To: David Thorne
Subject: Re: Re: Hey

Okay, I've booked you a single. What are you going to do for talent night?

From: David Thorne
Date: Monday 14 March 2011 3.04pm
To: Melissa Peters
Subject: Re: Re: Re: Hey

Probably a disappearing act with a bottle of scotch and a kayak. You?

From: Melissa Peters
Date: Monday 14 March 2011 3.08pm
To: David Thorne
Subject: Re: Re: Re: Re: Hey

I don't know yet. Probably a dance or something.

E34-F

From: Jennifer Haines
Date: Friday 12 October 2012 9.51am
To: David Thorne
Subject: Employee Self Evaluation Form

David,

Have you had a chance to complete the E34-F I left on your desk Monday? I told you I wanted these by the end of the week and it is now Friday afternoon. You are the only one who hasn't provided theirs yet.

Thank you, Jennifer

....

From: David Thorne
Date: Friday 12 October 2012 10.02am
To: Jennifer Haines
Subject: Re: Meeting this afternoon.

Morning Jen,

I'll have that to you in an hour. I was putting it off becasue I assumed some degree of non-delusional honesty was required, but, after reading Simon's self evaluation while he was out at lunch, I understand this is not the case.

David

Employee Self Evaluation Form

E34-F

Instructions for completing this form

Please complete this self evaluation form prior to your formal performance review and return to the Human Resources Department. Your answers will be discussed in your review session. Please retain a copy for your records. If you have any questions regarding the completion of this form, please see your supervisor or the Human Resources department.

Date Oct / 8 / 2012	**Employee Name** David Thorne
Job Title Copy writer / design director / office slut	
Department Design	**Supervisor** Geordi La Forge

Rating
Excellent Performs all tasks in an exceptional manner.
Good Performs many tasks well, all other tasks adequately and requires little supervision.
Satisfactory Performs all tasks satisfactorily and requires occasional supervision.
Unsatisfactory Fails to perform many tasks and requires regular supervision.

Office Use Only
Please do not write in this area.
☐ E30-A
☐ E30-B ok.

---

1. Procedures met Review procedures you have met during the last 12 months.

Comments My daily 10.30 procedure of watching Jodie consume cake while complaining about not being able to lose weight was met 70 percent of the time. I was absent the other 30% but I assume Jodie still ate cake. Her procedure of wearing stretchy bike-pants despite obviously having never been near a bike was also met.

☒ all of the above
☐ Excellent
☐ Good
☐ Satisfactory
☐ Unsatisfactory

---

2. Procedures implemented Review procedures you have implemented during the last 12 months

Comments I attempted to implement a daily procedure of co-worker bonding whereby we stop work half an hour before closing and spend 15 minutes insulting each other and then another 15 minutes apologising for the terrible things that were said. Staff enthusiasm and adoption of this procedure was disappointing.

☒ gift certicate
☐ Excellent
☐ Good
☐ Satisfactory
☐ Unsatisfactory

3. Objectives met Review objectives you have met during the last 12 months.

Comments My objective of having my monitor positioned where nobody else in the office could see it was met by rotating my desk two inches per day over a three month period so that nobody would notice. I also placed a plant on my desk to point at in case anyone asked, "is something different in here?"

- [x] select track
- [ ] Excellent
- [ ] Good
- [ ] Satisfactory
- [ ] Unsatisfactory

4. Future objectives Review future goals and objectives and your ability to execute these objectives.

Comments If you were to travel back in time to 1012 and show a 2012 John Deere combine harvester to a peasant working the King's land, he would think it was magic. It is therefore difficult to predict what the future will bring. Probably something to do with hover-belts or chickens that cook themselves when you press a button on their head.

- [x] robot servants
- [ ] Excellent
- [ ] Good
- [ ] Satisfactory
- [ ] Unsatisfactory

5. Time management Review your ability/strengths to meet project timelines over the last 12 months.

Comments My ability to construct viable excuses as to why client's projects have not been completed on time is one of my strengths. Usually, I am able to convince the client that it is their fault. If not, I tell them Simon is the one working on their project and we don't like to rush him or he slaps his head and screams.

- [x] included
- [ ] Excellent
- [ ] Good
- [ ] Satisfactory
- [ ] Unsatisfactory

6. Special skills/abilities Review any special skills and/or abilities you may have and how they are utilized.

Comments Telekinesis. The largest object I have been able to move by staring at and concentrating is a Bic pen but I practice at my desk for at least four hours per day on other objects. This would be useful if someone asked to borrow a pen and I was completely paralysed from a trampoline accident or spider bite.

- [x] yes
- [ ] Excellent
- [ ] Good
- [ ] Satisfactory
- [ ] Unsatisfactory

7. OH&S compliance Review office safety procedures you have met during the previous 12 months.

Comments When I run with scissors, I always point them away from me. Towards Simon. Also, when cleaning my handguns at work, I ensure that the safety is on and when descending stairs, I make sure to always hold onto the rail - especially if I am drunk or only wearing socks.

- [x] used item
- [ ] Excellent
- [ ] Good
- [ ] Satisfactory
- [ ] Unsatisfactory

8. Communication Review your ability to communicate with peers, supervisors and clients.

Comments In case I am ever captured and need to communicate with someone in an adjoining cell without the guards overhearing, I have taught myself Morse code. To bring others up to speed, I answer the phone by tapping on the mouthpiece. This skill will also be useful if we ever have clients who are triffids.

- [x] disable pop-ups
- [ ] Excellent
- [ ] Good
- [ ] Satisfactory
- [ ] Unsatisfactory

9. Training Review any training you have received or wish to receive and your application of this training.

Comments I would like to get my fork-lift license. I realise application would be limited to transferring Jill between her desk and the kitchen but if the business is paying for it, why not? You should also probably put me down for fencing, woodwork and kayaking. Also, I will probably need a raise with all these new skills.

- [x] free subscription
- [ ] Excellent
- [ ] Good
- [ ] Satisfactory
- [ ] Unsatisfactory

10. Work environment Review your work environment and any recommendations you may have.

Comments A total ban on Nickelback posters, photos of ugly children, and Jodie's bike-pants would be an improvement. As would some kind of rope ladder outside my window. I would also like Simon to wear a bag over his head and for me to be allowed to punch it. Also, if we moved his desk outside, it would give us more room for activities.

- [x] scented
- [ ] Excellent
- [ ] Good
- [ ] Satisfactory
- [ ] Unsatisfactory

11. Attendance Review your attendance record over the previous 12 months.

Comments	I have attended the office 100% of the time that I was not able to come up with a believable excuse for doing something else instead. If I lock my office door and shimmy out the window ten minutes after arriving, it still counts as attending and I actually get a lot more done this way; last week, I painted my outdoor furniture.	[x] family pack [ ] Excellent [ ] Good [ ] Satisfactory [ ] Unsatisfactory

12. Action plan Review any action plans you may have. These will be discussed during your review session.

Comments	The main character, a ten year old girl driven by revenge for the killing of her parents, trains as an assassin. There would be a lot of slow motion and maybe a suit that enhances her speed and skills that she builds because she is a genius and can read and memorise a whole book just by flicking through the pages.	[x] 2 thumbs up [ ] Excellent [ ] Good [ ] Satisfactory [ ] Unsatisfactory

13. Additional review Add any additional reviews you may wish to discuss during your review session.

Comments	Quite disappointed with this product, hence only giving it two stars; the handle broke off after using it once. I would recommend spending a little more on a quality product. Also, the colour is nothing like the product shown in the photo, the photo shows it as a deep blue and the product is more like a turquoise.	[ ] Excellent [ ] Good [ ] Satisfactory [ ] Unsatisfactory [x] send back

After completing this form
Please sign and date the completed self-evaluation form and return to the Human Resources Department.

Signed _David Thorne_   **Date** Oct / 8 / 2012

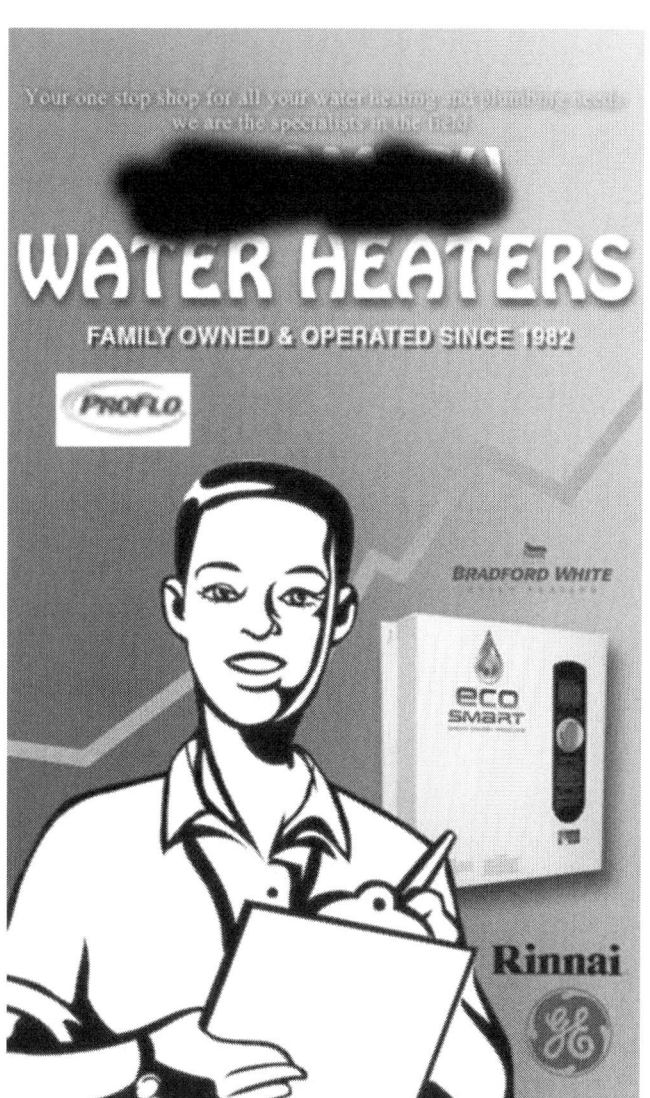

More Branded

Martin's staff profile includes the following bio which I suspect Martin may have written himself:

"Martin has a degree in fine arts and is a Windows expert. If you have a computer problem, Martin is your man. When he's not solving technical problems that nobody else can at work, he enjoys listening to live jazz, fishing and playing with his dog Tolkien."

Martin is also an aspiring graphic designer. His style can be likened to jazz in that only people like Martin think it's good.

Two weeks ago, I was commissioned by the company Martin works for to redesign their marketing materials. As the designer of their current brochure (shown left), Martin took the news surprisingly hard. While I commend anyone expressing creativity with whatever tools they have available, owning copies of Photoshop and InDesign does not make you a graphic designer.

I've owned a hammer for years but that doesn't mean I can build a house. I could probably give it a go but I'm not stupid enough to think it would be pleasant to look at or up to code. I did build a squirrel house recently though. It took me an entire week. Two weeks later it rained and the wood bowed and the nails popped out. I saw it collapse the other day and had to lift the roof off to free a rather annoyed squirrel.

From: Martin Buchanan
Date: Friday 8 Mar 2013 10.06am
To: David Thorne
Subject: Brochure

Hello. Louise asked me to send you the brochure files. I'm quite excited to see what changes we are making. Do you want the indesign files or just the text and images? If you are just changing the images I could do that here if you wanted. I know how to use Indesign.

From: David Thorne
Date: Friday 8 Mar 2013 10.13am
To: Martin Buchanan
Subject: Re: Brochure

Hello Martin,

Thank you for your email. While I appreciate the offer, I will not require any existing components for the redesign.

Regards, David

From: Martin Buchanan
Date: Friday 8 Mar 2013 10.25am
To: David Thorne
Subject: Re: Re: Brochure

Are you going to just make it more branded or redraw

everything? That seems like it would take a long time when I already have the files. Are you changing how things look? I don't think it needs a big change just the photos on the back need updating and the new web address.

Do you want me to copy and paste the text and the images into an email for your changes or do want to tell me what changes to make and I make them?

....

From: David Thorne
Date: Friday 8 Mar 2013 10.37am
To: Martin Buchanan
Subject: Re: Re: Re: Brochure

Hello Martin,

Your enthusiasm is commendable but I do not require any files from you at this stage.

I was commissioned to redesign the complete suite of marketing materials and this includes the brochure. If for some reason I do decide to use any of the existing graphic components, a quick search on Google for 'clipart of man holding clipboard' and 'blue wiggly line for no apparent reason' should suffice.

Regards, David

From: Martin Buchanan
Date: Friday 8 Mar 2013 10.51am
To: David Thorne
Subject: Re: Re: Re: Re: Brochure

The blue line represents growth, like on the stock market.

There's nothing wrong with the current design, it just needs to be more branded. If you add more brand without changing the design and update the photos it will be perfect.

Do you want me to send you the logo? Are you changing the text?

From: David Thorne
Date: Friday 8 Mar 2013 10.58am
To: Martin Buchanan
Subject: Re: Re: Re: Re: Re: Brochure

Hello Martin,

While I will be using segments of the current text - primarily the words 'and' and 'it' - the majority will be rewritten and the logo, which appears to have been created by someone with severe Apophenia, needs to be redrawn in a higher resolution than the current 6x8 pixels.

Regards, David

From: Martin Buchanan
Date: Friday 8 Mar 2013 11.18am
To: David Thorne
Subject: Re: Re: Re: Re: Re: Re: Brochure

No it doesn't. It prints fine.

What bits are you changing? You should just send the text changes to me and I will make them on the files. It doesn't make sense to change how the brochure looks too much.

We shouldn't be changing it at all, it's just a waste of money. We've still got four boxes of the current ones left downstairs. It would make more sense to print stickers and stick them over the old web address on the back. I designed that brochure and it's had a lot of good feedback.

....

From: David Thorne
Date: Friday 8 Mar 2013 11.36am
To: Martin Buchanan
Subject: Re: Re: Re: Re: Re: Re: Re: Brochure

Hello Martin,

Your mother stating, "That's nice dear" probably falls under the label of encouragement rather than feedback.

I often tell my offspring that he is talented despite the artwork on our refrigerator clearly illustrating the opposite. I commended him last week on an excellent representation of an octopus only to find out that it was meant to be a car.

Unfortunately, confidence through encouragement does not automatically equate to capability. If I were to use my offspring's artwork on a brochure for the Ford Motor Company, feedback comprising of, "Is that a fucking octopus?" would be far more likely than, "This will sell a lot of cars, just add some clipart of a man holding a clipboard and a blue wiggly line and it's good to go."

While some people might describe the current brochure as sophisticated, message driven, and on-brand, those people should be reminded that sarcasm is the lowest form of wit.

As a designer, I do understand attachment to something you have created and that other people's opinions are merely hurdles constructed of inanity, but as every component of a company's marketing materials define that company's brand message, which in this instance appears to be "look at how many different typefaces our computer has", the decision to hide them in the basement was probably a wise one.

Regards, David

From: Martin Buchanan
Date: Friday 8 Mar 2013 11.57am
To: David Thorne
Subject: Re: Re: Re: Re: Re: Re: Re: Re: Brochure

They're not hidden, they're on a shelf. Obviously you're going to say my design isn't very good so you can justify charging to redesign it.

Everyone who has seen the current brochure has said it is amazing. Ive got a degree in fine arts and I've done an advanced course in Adobe. I probably know more indesign than you do. Art is subjective.

I branded it to appeal to our customers, they don't want modern looking things.

From: David Thorne
Date: Friday 8 Mar 2013 12.19pm
To: Martin Buchanan
Subject: Re: Re: Re: Re: Re: Re: Re: Re: Brochure

Hello Martin,

Your company sells water heaters. I might be missing something but I fail to understand how stock market graphs and rainbow gradient backgrounds relate to warm showers.

While art is certainly subjective, it has also been said that art is a tryst, for in the joy of it, maker and beholder meet. Unfortunately, in this case, the tryst would be the emotional-connection equivalent of a quick handjob in a K-mart toilet from a middle-aged shelf-stacker named Rhonda in exchange for half a packet of Marlboro Menthol lights.

That's not to say the current design is completely without its merits. Running multi-colored drop-shadowed type to the very edges has effectively removed the need to fill in all that annoying negative space with more clipart and, using every color but your corporate color was a bold approach.

When Louise first handed me the brochure, I thought she was inviting me to a rave.

If nothing else, your style is certainly unique. During my twenty-odd years of working with professionals in the design industry, I can honestly say I have never seen anything quite like it. Once the redesign is completed, I am happy to send you a proof following pre-press and you are welcome to provide any suggestions you may have at that time.

Regards, David

From: Martin Buchanan
Date: Friday 8 Mar 2013 1.08pm
To: David Thorne
Subject: Re: Re: Re: Re: Re: Re: Re: Re: Re: Re: Brochure

Don't bother sending me a proof. I'm not going to be here next week and I'm not interested in seeing it or reading any more of your bullshit anyway. I'm busy organizing a fishing trip and leave tonight. Convincing people they need to redesign things when there is nothing wrong with what they have so you can make some quick cash just makes you a con artist.

Dropshadows lift the type off the page as if they are 3D. You probably don't even know how to do them. Have fun redoing the whole brochure without any files. While you're sitting at your desk redrawing everything next week, I will be relaxing in a chair with my new Shimano rod and laughing.

From: Louise Brown
Date: Friday 8 Mar 2013 3.22pm
To: David Thorne
Subject: Files

Hi David,

Just wondering if you received the brochure files. We have the photographer coming in on Monday so can hopefully get product shots to you mid week. Have a great weekend.

Louise

....

From: David Thorne
Date: Friday 8 Mar 2013 3.35pm
To: Louise Brown
Subject: Re: Files

Hello Louise,

Looking forward to seeing the photos.

I've been in contact with Martin but he has not yet sent any files. He's probably preoccupied with his upcoming fishing trip. If you could give him the following list of items I require before he leaves, that would be appreciated:

1 x rainbow gradient background, 36 x typefaces used, 1 x clipart of man holding a clipboard, 1 x image of wiggly blue line, 1 x logo in 6x8 pixel .gif format, and 1 x copy of his upcoming book *Drop-shadows. A Guide by Martin Buchanan.*

Thanks, David

From: Martin Buchanan
Date: Friday 8 Mar 2013 3.57pm
To: David Thorne
Subject: Fwd: Re: Files

I'm not sending you anything bitch.

....

From: David Thorne
Date: Friday 8 Mar 2013 4.38pm
To: Martin Buchanan
Subject: Re: Fwd: Re: Files

Dear Martin,

Understood. You are no doubt busy organising your upcoming fishing trip.

To help you out, I have whipped up the invite for you. It's based on your brochure design but I added clipart of two men shaking hands and a clock to represent time spent with friends because there was a bare spot in the bottom right corner.

Enjoy your break.

Regards, David

Attached Image: Fishingtrip.jpg

From: Martin Buchanan
Date: Friday 8 Mar 2013 4.50pm
To: David Thorne
Subject: Re: Re: Forwarded: Re: Files

I will. Enjoy sucking dick.

Interviews

A few weeks ago, the company I work for lost a designer. While in the middle of a client meeting - explaining to a rep from Kraft Foods why fourteen pages of text cannot fit on the back of 320mL jar label - Simon stood, stated, "I can't do this anymore," and left. His dramatic exit was diminished somewhat when, despite having opened and closed the boardroom door hundreds of times before, he pulled and shook the handle for several seconds yelling, "What the fuck is wrong with this door?" before remembering it swung outwards.

Earlier that week, Simon had confided to Melissa that he was having 'relationship issues' so everyone knew within an hour that his girlfriend had slept with a white-water rafting instructor.

Simon's father came in to collect his personal belongings a few days later and when I asked how Simon was doing, he replied, "He'll be fine, what doesn't kill you makes you stronger."

Which isn't always true as I know someone who contracted Ross River Virus several years ago and he needs to be pushed around in a wheelchair, moaning the whole time about his joints and inadequate ramp access. I visited him in his ground-floor apartment once but it was a miserable and forced conversation so I told him I had a present for him in the car and went to get it. Then drove home.

....

From: Mike Campbell
Date: Wednesday 4 June 2014 10.09am
To: David Thorne
Subject: Job interviews

David,

My flight is at 2pm today but I need to pack so I'll leave around 12. I fly back Tuesday morning. Jennifer is on annual leave so you and Kevin will have to hold the first round of interviews for the new designer in my absence. Please rearrange your schedule for Thursday and Friday to suit.

The resumes are on my desk in the blue folder. There are 7 interviews on Thursday and 6 on Friday. Ask Melissa to make sure the boardroom is clean and offer applicants coffee when they arrive. We're only selecting 5 for final interviews so let's get a good feel for fit. Please organize a list of 10 questions for the applicants before tomorrow and attach their answers to the top of each resume so I can go through them next week. What are their strengths and weaknesses? Are they proactive or reactive? etc.

Mike

From: David Thorne
Date: Wednesday 4 June 2014 10.26am
To: Mike Campbell
Subject: Re: Job interviews

Mike,

No problem. I will perform a Google search for 'modern interviewing techniques circa 1982' right away. The importance of determining which applicants are capable of providing contrived responses to stupid questions cannot be overstated. It is essentially the key to getting on well with everyone here.

It's possible, however, more could be learned, and a greater 'feel for fit' obtained, through open discussion. Perhaps over a beer.

I therefore suggest Kevin and I meet each applicant in the board room before proceeding to the local bar to chat. Or wait there and have Melissa give them directions.

David

From : Mike Campbell
Date : Wednesday 4 June 2014 10.55am
To : David Thorne
Subject : Re: Re: Job interviews

David,

All interviews will take place in the boardroom.

Asking set questions means I can rate the answers when I get back. What will I have to go on if you just chat?

It's going to be a busy month and we need to replace Simon immediately. With someone normal. The questions will help us avoid a repeat of last month's embarrassing drama.

I'm sorry he's having issues but people need to learn to leave their personal lives at the door. This isn't the Kardashians.

Mike

From : David Thorne
Date : Wednesday 4 June 2014 11.18am
To : Mike Campbell
Subject : Re: Re: Re: Job interviews

Mike,

I'm not sure what *Star Trek* has to do with any of this but embarrassing drama is standard operating procedure around here. Bringing someone normal into the fold would just be cruel.

Melissa isn't speaking to anyone because she just found out how much more Jennifer makes than her and Jennifer has gone emergency hat shopping due to her hairdresser cutting her bangs too short. As she left, I heard Melissa say to someone on the phone, "It must be nice to be able to afford hats."

I won't bother going into my own daily drama, but I'm fairly positive you're not going to like it. Kevin is the only 'normal' person here and that's because he gave up on having a personality when he discovered gardening. Nobody cares how your cabbages are doing, Kevin.

But yes, it is certainly possible that had Simon been asked what his weakness is prior to employment, that particular drama may have been avoided. When selecting final candidates from this week's interviews, we will immediately weed out those answering, "Dramatic things might happen during a client meeting if I ever find out my partner had sex with a white-water rafting instructor while away on holiday for three days."

Do we also discard the likes of, "If I ever go hiking on the edge of a volcano I might slip and fall into lava without backing up my work," or do these go in the 'maybe' pile with, "I've been known to get caught in open fields during lightning storms"?

Multiple-choice questions might streamline the process. This would provide a range of possible scenarios to preempt and serve as a score tally to go on. Should there be a draw, we can have the finalists guess the amount of jellybeans in a jar, and time how long it takes them to do twenty push-ups for bonus points. Any remaining interview time that would otherwise be wasted on chatting can be spent quietly avoiding eye contact.

In addition to those already suggested, are there any specific pointless questions you want included?

David

From: Mike Campbell
Date: Wednesday 4 June 2014 11.41am
To: David Thorne
Subject: Re: Re: Re: Re: Job interviews

How is this an issue?

Just ask 10 fucking interview questions. I don't care what they are as long as I have a record. And add notes so you can remember who they are.

Mike

Applicant Questionnaire

Name *Michelle Roper*

Day of Interview ☑ Thursday ☐ Friday   **Time of Interview** *4 PM*

1 How is this an issue?   *"It isn't. Go ahead."*

2 To evaluate strengths & weaknesses, please rate your chance of survival in the following situations:

Slipping on a rock, possibly while hiking, and falling into lava. *0* %

Building an enlargement ray and testing it on a flower but a bee gets caught in the beam and turns to the size of a bus and stings you in the face. *20* %

Being kidnapped while back-packing across Europe and having a German scientist sew your mouth onto the rectum of another back-packer. *10* %

Taking several rattlesnake bites to the neck. *0* %

Exploding. Note, you are not wearing safety glasses at the time. *0* %

3 Have you ever been caught in an open field during a lightning storm? ☐ Yes ☑ No
If yes, were you holding a shovel? ☐ Yes ☐ No

4 Are you Proactive or Reactive? ☑ Yes ☐ No

5 Has your partner ever shown an interest in white-water rafting? ☐ Yes ☑ No

6 Have you ever thought about what you would 'invent' to survive and prosper if you fell through a time portal and found yourself in Medieval England during the 11th century? ☑ Yes ☐ No

7 If you could be any member of the Kardassian family, which one would you choose?
☐ Willis ☐ Arnold ☑ Kimberly ☐ Mr Huxtable

8 Have you ever considered growing your own cabbage? ☐ Yes ☑ No

9 There is a type of parasite that takes control of an ant's brain and makes it climb a blade of grass to wait for a hungry cow. The parasite then reproduces in the cow's lower intestine. When the cow drops its faeces, the parasites wait for ants to approach and the circle continues.
Working in the design & advertising industry is most like being:
☐ The Ant
☐ The Cow
☑ The Parasite
☐ The Faeces

10 If you knew a spell to summon Jesus, what would you use your one wish for?
☑ Infinite wishes ☐ A new car ☐ To be an eagle ☐ Cake

Additional Notes
Short lesbian wearing a Blondie t-shirt.
Excellent portfolio.   ★ Recommend for
Good communication.   final interview. ★

Applicant Questionnaire

Name Wayne Redding

Day of Interview ☐ Thursday ☑ Friday   **Time of Interview** 10:AM

1 How is this an issue? *"I don't have an issue, I'm just nervous."*

2 To evaluate strengths & weaknesses, please rate your chance of survival in the following situations:

Slipping on a rock, possibly while hiking, and falling into lava. __10__ %

Building an enlargement ray and testing it on a flower but a bee gets caught in the beam and turns to the size of a bus and stings you in the face. __50__ %

Being kidnapped while back-packing across Europe and having a German scientist sew your mouth onto the rectum of another back-packer. __25__ %

Taking several rattlesnake bites to the neck. __5__ %

Exploding. Note, you are not wearing safety glasses at the time. __0__ %

3 Have you ever been caught in an open field during a lightning storm? ☐ Yes ☑ No
If yes, were you holding a shovel? ☐ Yes ☐ No

4 Are you Proactive or Reactive? ☐ Yes ☐ No *"I don't follow politics."*

5 Has your partner ever shown an interest in white-water rafting? ☐ Yes ☑ No

6 Have you ever thought about what you would 'invent' to survive and prosper if you fell through a time portal and found yourself in Medieval England during the 11th century? ☑ Yes ☐ No

7 If you could be any member of the Kardassian family, which one would you choose?
☐ Willis ☑ Arnold ☐ Kimberly ☐ Mr Huxtable

8 Have you ever considered growing your own cabbage? ☐ Yes ☑ No

9 There is a type of parasite that takes control of an ant's brain and makes it climb a blade of grass to wait for a hungry cow. The parasite then reproduces in the cow's lower intestine. When the cow drops its faeces, the parasites wait for ants to approach and the circle continues.
Working in the design & advertising industry is most like being:
☐ The Ant
☑ The Cow
☐ The Parasite
☐ The Faeces

10 If you knew a spell to summon Jesus, what would you use your one wish for?
☐ Infinite wishes ☑ A new car ☐ To be an eagle ☐ Cake

Additional Notes

Wayne was 15 minutes late and covered in sweat. He missed the bus so ran here. In a suit. Regardless, excellent portfolio. Nice hat. Breeds green tree frogs.

★ Recommend final interview.

Applicant Questionnaire

Name Emily Bennett

Day of Interview ☐ Thursday ☑ Friday **Time of Interview** 11 AM

1 How is this an issue? *"What? No, I was just scratching my nose."*

2 To evaluate strengths & weaknesses, please rate your chance of survival in the following situations:

Slipping on a rock, possibly while hiking, and falling into lava. __5__ %

Building an enlargement ray and testing it on a flower but a bee gets caught in the beam and turns to the size of a bus and stings you in the face. __0__ %

Being kidnapped while back-packing across Europe and having a German scientist sew your mouth onto the rectum of another back-packer. __0__ %

Taking several rattlesnake bites to the neck. __10__ %

Exploding. Note, you are not wearing safety glasses at the time. __0__ %

3 Have you ever been caught in an open field during a lightning storm? ☐ Yes ☑ No
If yes, were you holding a shovel? ☐ Yes ☐ No

4 Are you Proactive or Reactive? ☑ Yes ☐ No

5 Has your partner ever shown an interest in white-water rafting? ☐ Yes ☑ No

6 Have you ever thought about what you would 'invent' to survive and prosper if you fell through a time portal and found yourself in Medieaval England during the 11th century? ☐ Yes ☑ No

7 If you could be any member of the Kardassian family, which one would you choose?
☐ Willis ☐ Arnold ☑ Kimberly ☐ Mr Huxtable

8 Have you ever considered growing your own cabbage? ☑ Yes ☐ No

9 There is a type of parasite that takes control of an ant's brain and makes it climb a blade of grass to wait for a hungry cow. The parasite then reproduces in the cow's lower intestine. When the cow drops its faeces, the parasites wait for ants to approach and the circle continues.
Working in the design & advertising industry is most like being:
☑ The Ant
☐ The Cow
☐ The Parasite
☐ The Faeces

10 If you knew a spell to summon Jesus, what would you use your one wish for?
☑ Infinite wishes ☐ A new car ☐ To be an eagle ☐ Cake

Additional Notes Rode a bike to the interview. Parked it in the foyer so it wouldn't be stolen. Solid portfolio. Very friendly and bright.

✱ Recommend for final interview.

Applicant Questionnaire

Name Hoahan Nguyen

Day of Interview ☑ Thursday ☐ Friday **Time of Interview** 1 PM

1 How is this an issue? *"How is what an issue?"*

2 To evaluate strengths & weaknesses, please rate your chance of survival in the following situations:
- Slipping on a rock, possibly while hiking, and falling into lava. __10__%
- Building an enlargement ray and testing it on a flower but a bee gets caught in the beam and turns to the size of a bus and stings you in the face. __0__%
- Being kidnapped while back-packing across Europe and having a German scientist sew your mouth onto the rectum of another back-packer. __15__%
- Taking several rattlesnake bites to the neck. __10__%
- Exploding. Note, you are not wearing safety glasses at the time. __0__%

3 Have you ever been caught in an open field during a lightning storm? ☐ Yes ☑ No
If yes, were you holding a shovel? ☐ Yes ☐ No

4 Are you Proactive or Reactive? ☑ Yes ☐ No

5 Has your partner ever shown an interest in white-water rafting? ☐ Yes ☑ No

6 Have you ever thought about what you would 'invent' to survive and prosper if you fell through a time portal and found yourself in Medieaval England during the 11th century? ☐ Yes ☑ No

7 If you could be any member of the Kardassian family, which one would you choose?
☐ Willis ☐ Arnold ☑ Kimberly ☐ Mr Huxtable

8 Have you ever considered growing your own cabbage? ☐ Yes ☑ No

9 There is a type of parasite that takes control of an ant's brain and makes it climb a blade of grass to wait for a hungry cow. The parasite then reproduces in the cow's lower intestine. When the cow drops its faeces, the parasites wait for ants to approach and the circle continues.
Working in the design & advertising industry is most like being:
☑ The Ant
☐ The Cow
☐ The Parasite
☐ The Faeces

10 If you knew a spell to summon Jesus, what would you use your one wish for?
☐ Infinite wishes ☑ A new car ☐ To be an eagle ☐ Cake

Additional Notes
Thin eyes. Possibly Asian.
Portfolio is exceptional - very clean design.
Good communication. ✱ Recomend for final interview.

Applicant Questionnaire

Name Walter Bowens

Day of Interview ☐ Thursday ☑ Friday **Time of Interview** 2 : 00

1 How is this an issue? "*Is that one of the questions?*"

2 To evaluate strengths & weaknesses, please rate your chance of survival in the following situations:

Slipping on a rock, possibly while hiking, and falling into lava. __30__ %

Building an enlargement ray and testing it on a flower but a bee gets caught in the beam and turns to the size of a bus and stings you in the face. __30__ %

Being kidnapped while back-packing across Europe and having a German scientist sew your mouth onto the rectum of another back-packer. __70__ %

Taking several rattlesnake bites to the neck. __20__ %

Exploding. Note, you are not wearing safety glasses at the time. __0__ %

3 Have you ever been caught in an open field during a lightning storm? ☑ Yes ☐ No
If yes, were you holding a shovel? ☐ Yes ☑ No

4 Are you Proactive or Reactive? ☐ Yes ☑ No

5 Has your partner ever shown an interest in white-water rafting? ☐ Yes ☑ No

6 Have you ever thought about what you would 'invent' to survive and prosper if you fell through a time portal and found yourself in Medieaval England during the 11th century? ☐ Yes ☑ No

7 If you could be any member of the Kardassian family, which one would you choose?
☐ Willis ☐ Arnold ☐ Kimberly ☑ Mr Huxtable

8 Have you ever considered growing your own cabbage? ☑ Yes ☐ No

9 There is a type of parasite that takes control of an ant's brain and makes it climb a blade of grass to wait for a hungry cow. The parasite then reproduces in the cow's lower intestine. When the cow drops its faeces, the parasites wait for ants to approach and the circle continues.
Working in the design & advertising industry is most like being:
☑ The Ant
☐ The Cow
☐ The Parasite
☐ The Faeces

10 If you knew a spell to summon Jesus, what would you use your one wish for?
☐ Infinite wishes ☑ A new car ☐ To be an eagle ☐ Cake

Additional Notes
Came to interview wearing cargo shorts. Nice kid.
Excellent portfolio - has worked on good projects. Talked to Kevin for 20 minutes about cabbages. ✱ Recommend for final interview. ✱

From : Mike Campbell
Date : Tuesday 10 June 2014 12.21pm
To : David Thorne
Cc: Kevin Eastwood
Subject : No subject

David,

Can I see you and Kevin in my office please?

Mike

Product Naming

"We should call it the 'Power Washer'."

"That's what it is, Walter. Pressure washers are also known as 'power washers'."

"Bullshit. I've never heard anyone call it a 'power' washer."

"The term 'power washing' is interchangeable with 'pressure washing'; like couch and sofa."

"'Power Washer 5000' then. Because it has 5000 psi of pressures."

"The packaging will include the description '5000psi Pressure Washer'. It's like naming a four slice toaster 'Toaster 4, 4 slice toaster'."

"No, it isn't. What's your suggestion then?"

"I've made a short list but am leaning towards 'Torrent.'"

"Pfft. What's a pressure washer got to do with downloading movies?"

Kenneth's Meetings

There's a lot that could be said about Kenneth but none of it is interesting so I'll keep it to one paragraph. I once slept for twenty minutes during one of his meetings and when I awoke, he was explaining the same pie chart that I'd nodded off to. I looked around the boardroom to see if anyone had noticed and two other people were asleep. Melissa, our secretary, actually had her mouth open with a line of spittle running down to the table. I poked a pen in her mouth and she gagged and woke up startled, which I found pretty amusing. I chuckled through the rest of the meeting and for an hour or two afterwards whenever I thought about it. It was the most entertaining thing that has ever happened in one of Kenneth's meetings.

From: Kenneth Warner
Date: Monday 6 August 2018 10.16am
To: David Thorne
Subject: Meeting

David, you missed the meeting this morning. Can we reschedule that for 3pm please?

Ken

From: David Thorne
Date: Monday 6 August 2018 10.22am
To: Kenneth Warner
Subject: Re: Meeting

Kenneth,

That won't be possible as I've decided not to attend any more of your meetings. They're like boredom taking on physical form and punching you in the face until you black out.

David

From: Kenneth Warner
Date: Monday 6 August 2018 10.27am
To: David Thorne
Subject: Re: Re: Meeting

David,

I don't give a flying fuck what you've decided.
I've rescheduled the meeting for 3pm and I expect you to be there.

Ken

From: David Thorne
Date: Monday 6 August 2018 10.41am
To: Kenneth Warner
Subject: Auto responder

Thank you for your email.

I'm currently out of the office but will reply to your email upon my return. If you require assistance during my absence, please contact Kenneth. He will be happy to arrange a meeting, as it's all he does. Last week we had fourteen meetings. Seven of which were to discuss where we are on projects, five were to discuss why we are behind on projects, two were to discuss the importance of meeting deadlines, and one was about mouse droppings in the kitchen which turned out to be burnt rice.

Regards, David

From: Kenneth Warner
Date: Monday 6 August 2018 10.50am
To: David Thorne
Subject: Re: Auto responder

I saw you close your blinds. There were a total of 9 meetings last week, not 14, and you didn't attend 4 of them. We're having a meeting at 3pm. Gary from Emerson is expecting an update on the pressure washer packaging and I need to know where we are with the project. Also, as you are fully aware, I prefer Ken thank you.

Ken

From: David Thorne
Date: Monday 6 August 2018 10.58am
To: Kenneth Warner
Subject: Emerson packaging update

Kenneth,

Packaging is completed pending revised copy from Ben.

Gary signed off on the name *Torrent 5000* and product decals were approved last week. You can let him know that he will receive a proof for the packaging by Wednesday.

David

From: Kenneth Warner
Date: Monday 6 August 2018 11.22am
To: David Thorne
Subject: Re: Emerson packaging update

Thank you for the update but I'd still like to have a meeting at 3pm.

Ken

From: David Thorne
Date: Monday 6 August 2018 11.43am
To: Kenneth Warner
Subject: Re: Re: Emerson packaging update

Kenneth,

Of course you would. Without a meeting to schedule, attend or preside over, you shrivel like a forgotten carrot at the back of a crisper drawer.

The fact that a two-minute email is more productive than a meeting doesn't matter. An email doesn't allow you to point at things and repeat what's just been said in an irrelevant and annoying manner or provide you a captive audience for monologue from *Aimless: An Evening with Kenneth.*

We also don't get to find out what everyone did on the weekend, how much Jennifer's bathroom is going to cost to remodel, or why Walter decided to get his hair cut a little shorter this time.

I understand you get bored but have you considered a hobby? You're like an old lady who walks to the post office each day to buy a single stamp so she has someone to talk to about her cat that died in 1947.

I have two projects to be completed today and you're up to date with the Emerson packaging, so what exactly is the point of having another meeting?

David

From: Kenneth Warner
Date: Monday 6 August 2018 12.50pm
To: David Thorne
Subject: Re: Update

I don't appreciate being called a carrot or an old lady.

Just so you know, I intend to have a meeting with Mike and Jennifer to discuss your attitude and why you continually try to make my job harder.

Ken

From: David Thorne
Date: Monday 6 August 2018 1.13pm
To: Kenneth Warner
Subject: Re: Re: Update

Kenneth,

Nobody is trying to make your job harder. I realize you have a busy schedule of chair swiveling and pen tapping to get through. Those mines aren't going to sweep themselves and online quizzes about what kind of donut you are won't be accurate unless you take the time to answer each question honestly. We can't all be pink icing with sprinkles, Kenneth, someone has to be the plain donut.

David

From: Kenneth Warner
Date: Monday 6 August 2018 1.39pm
To: David Thorne
Subject: Re: Re: Re: Update

I'm speaking to Jennifer and Mike about this. I've had enough of you and your whole fucking department and am going to file a complaint.

Ken

From: Jennifer Haines
Date: Monday 6 August 2018 2.27pm
To: David Thorne **CC:** Kenneth Warner
Subject: F26-A

David, I'm cc'ing Ken on this email.

1. Please make yourself available for meetings. Communication between departments allows both parties to perform their job to the best of their abilities.

2. Personal insults are not permissible in the workplace.

Rather than lodge a complaint, I'd prefer we all met to discuss the issue like adults.

Would 4pm today work for you?

Thank you, Jennifer

From: David Thorne
Date: Monday 6 August 2018 2.35pm
To: Jennifer Haines **CC.** Kenneth Warner
Subject: Re: F26-A

Jennifer,

I'd rather you just lodged the complaint to be honest. I'm sure Ken has a fractal boner over the prospect of a meeting to discuss missed meetings but I have actual work to complete. I will apologize to him for the insults.

David

From: David Thorne
Date: Monday 6 August 2018 2.48pm
To: Kenneth Warner
Subject: Apology

Kenneth,

I'm sorry for calling you a plain donut, a shriveled carrot, and an old woman buying stamps.

David

From: Kenneth Warner
Date: Monday 6 August 2018 3.07pm
To: David Thorne
Subject: Re: Apology

Apology not accepted.

Mess with the bull, you get the horns.

Ken

Kenneth's Horns

From: David Thorne
Date: Friday 10 August 2018 2.06pm
To: Kenneth Warner
Subject: Emerson contract proof

Kenneth,

Emerson packaging proof for the pressure washer was signed off on Wednesday. I have the cromolyn (contract proof) in my office if you'd like to see it.

David

From: Kenneth Warner
Date: Friday 10 August 2018 2.17pm
To: David Thorne
Subject: Re: Emerson contract proof

Sorry, but I'm afraid I can't go in your office because it's like being punched by boredom coming to life.

Ken

Production Meeting

It was Jennifer's idea to add a suggestion box to the office. She probably read about it on a HR website's "*top ten list of sad and annoying things to do in the office that give the impression you're not just shopping online all day.*" Suggestion boxes are intended, I suppose, as an opportunity for employees to participate in decision making and thus feel empowered, assuming more ownership of their work environment. It showed the company cared, that feedback from staff was welcome and valued.

"Isn't that what these weekly production meetings are for?" I asked, "along with general gossip, tantrums and throwing people under a bus?"

The weekly half-hour production meeting in the boardroom was meant to ensure everyone was up-to-date and onboard with project progress and requirements. Being that our department was relatively small, however, everyone had a general idea of what everyone else was working on so focus moved quickly from pretending you were on top of things - or calling out others as the cause of not being on top of things - to who didn't receive a rose on *The Bachelor* the night before, iPhone case comparison, and updates from Kevin on how well his vegetable garden is doing.

'Well, yes, in part," agreed Jennifer, "but a suggestion box is anonymous. Some individuals might be hesitant to make suggestions during meetings for fear of those suggestions being belittled or thought of as stupid."

"So it's a special box just for stupid suggestions?"

"There are no stupid suggestions."

"What if someone suggests we all wear hats made out of bees? I'd need to be issued an EpiPen as I'm highly allergic."

"If you want to place a suggestion in the suggestion box about hats made of bees, that's up to you. I'd like to think that most people will add realistic suggestions that actually aim to improve workplace conditions. For the benefit of the person making the suggestion *and* others."

"Why would I suggest hats made out of bees? I was just making a point. I'm not sure how you'd even get the bees to stay in a hat shape. Plus it would be a bit annoying. Will there be prizes?"

"For what?"

"For coming up with the best suggestion. As an incentive of sorts. That way, every time someone places a suggestion in the suggestion box, it would be like entering a contest. We could give away a ham or something."

"Creating a better work environment *is* the incentive. Besides, it's anonymous, that's the point, there's no way to know who made each suggestion. Do you actually have anything constructive to add to this meeting?"

"No."

"No, I didn't think so."

A Zappo's shoe box was selected as the suggestion box. A hole was cut in the lid to facilitate speedy suggestion deposit and the words 'Suggestion Box' written on the side just in case anyone forgot what it was. Our creative director, Mike, complained that the boardroom table wasn't the place for an ugly Zappo's shoebox so Melissa added decoupage. Cutting pictures out of magazines and sticking them on with spray adhesive gave her something to do for three or four hours and nobody dared suggest that faces of babies in the middle of sunflowers looked a lot worse than the original Zappos logo.

"That's looking good. Very colourful."
"It's not finished yet, David. I still have to apply a varnish."
"Gloss or matte?"
"Gloss."
"Nice. Where'd you find all the baby faces?"
"It's only two different babies, I made colour photocopies of them so it looks like there's more. I needed one for the middle of each sunflower."
"Yes, the babies faces in the middle of sunflowers theme wouldn't have made sense if some of the sunflowers didn't have babies faces."
"Exactly."
"You've covered up the words 'Suggestion Box' though. What's to stop someone mistaking it for sewing supplies?"
"What?"
"Cotton spools and pincushions, that kind of thing, probably buttons."

"It's got a slot in the lid. For suggestions. Why would a box of sewing supplies have a slot in the lid?"

"It wouldn't, you're right. The sewing supplies would fall out if you shook the box vigorously. I don't know what I was thinking."

"I might add the words 'Suggestion Box' though."

"Maybe you could make the letters out of tiny baby faces using the 200% reduction setting on the photocopier. From a distance, they'd appear to be normal letters but up close, you'd realise that all the letters are made up of babies faces. Or their arms."

"That's way too much work, I'll probably just cut the letters out of a magazine."

"Like on a ransom note?"

"Yes, but friendlier."

It might be assumed that such an objet d'art, set on a design agency's boardroom table between a stack of *Logo Lounge* books and a concrete pot containing plastic grass, would, at the very least, result in someone raising an eyebrow and saying, "hmm." Or men in containment suits being sent in to secure the building. People don't 'put things somewhere' in design agencies, things are placed. Things that please the eye and balance the room. There are no walnut display cabinets containing ceramic horse figurines and margarita glasses shaped like cactus. Melissa's things, however, go wherever the fuck she wants them to go. With her 'eye for design' matched by her ability to take criticism, it's best for all concerned to simply block them out.

Once, in a moment of distraction, I suggested that certain office Christmas decorations - orange and yellow streamers hung across a stairwell - were, "kind of in the way and more autumnal than Christmassy." When I went to my car that afternoon, both side mirrors were missing. I found one in a bush but it was cracked so both had to be replaced. I tried comparing fingerprints left on the mirror to prints on Melissa's monitor screen but apparently two pieces of sticky tape featuring slightly similar swirly smears isn't enough evidence for disciplinary action.

A few months back, Melissa hung a framed painting, of two ladies in Victorian attire holding umbrellas, between two advertising awards on the wall of the boardroom. It was an extreme move that screamed, 'bring it on', but nobody did. It wasn't actually that bad of a painting but then it's pretty hard to fuck up a Paint by Numbers kit. You just have to have a steady hand and clean your brushes regularly.

A month before, Jennifer signed the office up for a five kilometre staff walk to promote Alzheimer's Awareness Week. Jennifer's father suffered from it so we all feigned caring. Apparently he'd once caught a taxi to the airport and waited fourteen hours for his wife, who had died several years earlier, to come out of the women's bathroom. Which is a bit sad but at least he's not putting cats in ovens and we've all had to wait outside of airport bathrooms. I figured I'd stroll along with everyone for a bit, fall behind, and go home. I'm not capable of walking five kilometres.

I could probably manage on a bike if it was all downhill but I wouldn't because there'd be no way of getting back and I don't ride bikes because I'm not ten. Melissa was assigned the task of organizing team t-shirts featuring the company name and logo for us to wear on the day. Apparently the website was confusing or something because she ordered coffee mugs.

I made a point of taking and walking with mine, holding it up as if to say 'cheers' each time Melissa looked my way but that got old surprisingly quickly and the mug was annoying to carry so I left it in someone's letter box. I'd like to think the person who checked their mail that day was delighted to find a free yellow mug with *Your Company Logo Here* emblazoned across it. It was a pretty big mug so perhaps they use it to eat soup out of.

"Margaret, have you seen my big yellow mug? The one I got in the mail?"
"It's in the dishwasher."
"Oh no, I was going to have some soup."
"We have soup bowls."
"Yes, but I didn't want a whole bowl of soup, just a big mug."
"What about the stoneware pottery mugs? They're pretty big."
"No, they're too gritty. I'll just go without."

I realise ordering big yellow mugs instead of t-shirts doesn't have anything to do with 'artistic touches' but it does show a lack of attention to detail. Possibly flagrant disregard. I don't know how it's even possible to accidentally order coffee mugs instead of t-shirts. Melissa said she had several windows open in her browser but why was one of them for big yellow mugs? Our corporate colour is a dusty green. I had a look at the website and it's not possible to order twelve t-shirts of various sizes with one click, you have to order the large, medium, small and Kevin's XL separately. Plus, the big yellow mugs came in packs of four which means the number 9* had to have been typed in the quantity box to total the thirty-six received. It just doesn't make any sense.

"David, the client was expecting their stationery by this morning. Did you place an order with the printer for their four-thousand letterheads, two-hundred business cards, one-thousand with-comps slips and six-hundred gusset folders?"
"Yes."
"Well, apparently they've just received eighteen tractor tires. Really big ones. Do you have any explanation for this?"
"I had several windows open in my browser."
"No problem, I'll let them know."

I originally had the number 11 here after asking my partner Holly what 36 divided by 4 was but then I remembered she's terrible at math and I checked on a calculator. I once cut 4 inches from the legs of our dining table based on Holly's calculations which turned out to be 3.6 inches out. When we sat at the table to test it, our knees were higher than the top. I ended up taking 3.6 inches from the chairs to fix the issue but it's like dining at a dwarf's house so we eat in bed now.

Mike tapped a folder in front of him with his Montblanc and looked around the boardroom table, "Does anyone have anything to discuss before we go over projects?"

Most of the design department was present for the weekly meeting. Jodie and Rebecca, apparently best friends now after a falling out the week before over a Facebook post about sandals, stopped comparing iWatch straps and looked around. Ben, sitting between Melissa and Jennifer instead of his usual place beside me, shook his head without looking up from his phone. Sitting in a different spot sent a strong message, a message that declared, "That's right, this is what happens if you describe copy I've written for toaster packaging as 'a bit wordy', I sit way over here. How ya like them apples?" Kevin sat in Ben's usual place. His brown polyester pants, pleats puffed out as if hiding a pumpkin, made swishing noises every time he moved. Walter, the youngest and newest member of the team, raised a hand.

"You don't have to raise your hand, Walter, what is it?"
"How long do you think this meeting will go for because I have a doctor's appointment at ten."
"Again? What did you even come in for?"
"To tell you I've got a doctor's appointment."
"Couldn't you have just rang and told Melissa?"
"I don't have any credit on my phone."
Mike sighed and took off his reading glasses, "Melissa, can you see about getting Walter a company phone? Who the fuck has a prepaid phone nowadays?"

Walter pumped a fist, "Awesome! Can I have the iPhone Plus?"

"No you fucking can't," replied Mike. He turned to Melissa, "Get him the smallest phone they have. He's not having a bigger phone than me."

Melissa made a note in her diary. The company issued everyone diaries, they were black leather bound with an embossed logo. She'd decorated hers with puff-paint. Walter sat back in his chair, arms crossed, looking dejected.

"And get me an iPhone Plus," Mike added, "Does anyone else have anything they'd like to bring up? Yes, Jodie?"

"There's ants in the kitchen area again," Jodie stated, glancing in my direction, "People should wipe down the counter if they spill sugar."

I'm not sure what happens but sometimes when I'm adding a teaspoon of sugar to my coffee, my hand does a little wiggle twitch thing and I miss the mug. It's not often that it happens, just when I'm least expecting it, but as I drink around twenty cups of coffee per day, not often is more often than you'd expect and when it does happen, I figure there's a chance it might happen again so there's really not much point cleaning up until then.

"How many ants?" I asked.
"I don't know," Jodie answered, "I didn't count them."
"A rough estimate will do."
"Three or four."
"So probably one."

"No, there were at least two."

"So three or four was a *very* rough estimate?"

"There shouldn't be *any* ants in the kitchen. Clean up your mess when you make one."

"Yes," piped in Rebecca, "I agree. It's common courtesy to other people who use the kitchen."

Most of Rebecca's conversations begin with, "Jodie and I both think…" and Jodie's with, "I've spoken to Rebecca about it and she agrees…" It's a symbiotic relationship that converts bitching into supported facts.

"Okay, fine," I conceded, "Sometimes when I add sugar to my coffee, my hand does a little wiggle twitch thing and I miss the cup. I'll clean it up in future. Does anyone else get that? The wiggle twitch thing?"

"Like Michael J. Fox?" asked Walter.

I frowned, "No, not like Michael J. Fox. He has full-blown Parkinsons."

"That probably started with a wiggle twitch thing," Walter suggested.

"It's not Parkinsons, Walter."

"How do you know? Have you been tested for it?"

"Yes, I went to a doctor and said, 'Sometimes I miss my coffee mug with a spoon of sugar so I'd like to be placed in one of those big magnet machines and be tested for Parkinson's please.'"

"MRI."

"Sorry?"

"Magnetic Resonance Imaging."

"Yes, one of those. I had to wear a gown. While I was in it, lighting struck the building and the MRI exploded. Now I can hear colours."

"That never happened."

"Can we get back to the meeting, please?" requested Mike, "I've got a busy day ahead of me so if nobody else... are we boring you, Ben?"

Ben looked up from his phone, "No, I'm listening. There's ants in the kitchen because David has Parkinson's. I'm capable of doing two things at once."

"Really? How's the Clairol copy coming along?"

"Good."

"Good as in 'finished?'"

"I'm working on it."

"It's a fucking shampoo bottle. How many different ways can there possibly be to say it makes your hair smell like coconut and Tiaré flower?"

"It's not *quite* that simple. I have to research Polynesian island culture."

"Yes, of course you do."

"Which is what I'm doing on my phone. If this was Ogilvy, they'd fly me there."

"Right, well I highly doubt that but why don't you fuck off to Ogilvy and ask them for a ticket?"

"Maybe I will."

"Good. Can you at least turn off key clicks? It sounds like someone sending morse code."

"Fine."

"Where are we on the artwork, David?"

While redirecting blame is a common practice in most companies, agencies have it down to a fine art. Throwing others under a bus is a skill-set listed on every designer's resumé - along with 'complaining about changes (advanced level)', 'that's not how I would have done it (advanced level 5)', and 'if they'd listened to me, it would have been heaps better (advanced level 18, gold medalist)'.

"Waiting on copy," I told Mike.
"Jesus Christ. I've got a meeting with Clairol on Tuesday, what am I meant to tell them?"
"That you're really excited at how it's progressing and can't wait to see their reaction?"
"Yes, probably, how are we doing on the Breville packaging?"
"Waiting on copy."
"Are you kidding? Do we need to fly you to Toaster Island, Ben?"
"I sent him copy," Ben replied sullenly, "It's not my fault he sent it back for changes."
"Oh, that was the toaster box copy?" I asked, "my mistake, Mister Dickens, I assumed it was your latest manuscript. I'll have Walter whack it on as it is. We can either use 2pt type or put the product photo on an inside flap."
"It was less than four paragraphs."
"It's a toaster. The product description calls for dot points, not plot twists."
"Dot points are a refuge for the illiterate."
"And a dot point in time saves nine. Anyone can change quotes to suit, Ben. Nobody's settling into a comfy chair by

the window on a rainy afternoon with a hot mug of cocoa and Oprah's toaster box of the month."

"Maybe they should."

"Alright Ben," Mike sighed, "cut it down to four or five dot points and have it to David by this afternoon."

"Fine, but it means putting the Clairol copy on hold. Or perhaps you'd like that as dot points as well?"

I nodded, "That works."

Ben twitched, "I wouldn't have to put up with this at Ogilvy."

Ben wouldn't survive ten minutes at Ogilvy. None of us would. They probably record hours and expect completed timesheets containing more than coffee stains and scribbles to get your pen working.

A few years back, a coworker named Simon convinced me to play paintball. It was for his nephew's birthday and they needed to make up the numbers required for a team. I met Simon at the venue and he introduced me to his teenage nephew, four of the nephew's gaming friends, and his girlfriend Cathy - a short chubby gothic with only one hand. I'd seen a photo of her and Simon but they'd had their arms around each other so the stump wasn't evident. I learned later she'd lost the hand as a child in an Insinkerator accident which is pretty much the worst way I can image losing a hand... actually, I thought about it and came up with several worse ways but most involved spider eggs hatching so I thought it best not to list them here. Cathy still had a nub, and a smaller nub on that which was half a thumb, but it wasn't much use due to tendon and nerve damage. To be honest, it would have been a lot less creepy if she'd just lost the whole thing and worn a rubber hand or something. I shook the nub when I met her without shuddering, which I feel was pretty mature and accepting of me. It was squishy like a sausage. She was wearing some kind of purple velvet dress that ended just above her knees, striped black & white knee-high stockings, and cherry Doc's with four-inch soles. I thought there might be a bit of running around that day so I'd dressed in cargo shorts, t-shirt and sneakers. Simon was wearing a red Adidas track suit, purchased a decade earlier during a hip-hop phase, while the teens all wore skinny jeans and *Call of Duty* t-shirts - apart from one in a Minecraft singlet who mustn't have got the memo. After signing waivers and being instructed on how to use the masks and paintball guns, the eight of us were sent into a room with benches to wait for the other team to arrive. We probably should have used that time to discuss strategy but I doubt it would have made a difference. There was a game still in progress when the other team arrived. They entered and waited with us, sitting across the room on facing benches. All eight were dressed head to toe in full military combat gear. Insignia on their shoulders showed a howling wolf silhouetted against a burning moon. They owned their own paintball guns.

"So you guys have played this before?" I asked.
One of them nodded and whispered something to the others.

"We're pretty much fucked, aren't we?" I added.
They all nodded silently.
"Probably should have worn more padding..."

An orange light lit up above the doorway and our teams were ushered into holding areas at opposite ends of a large warehouse. There was scaffolding, barricades and graffitied car bodies between us. A buzzer sounded, the lights dimmed, and the holding area door opened. With no game plan, we ran for cover behind barricades and waited. It was very quiet. I could hear myself and others breathing heavily. Had the other team even entered yet? I leant towards Simon to ask and saw his head snap violently back, engulfed in green splatter from at least five paintballs striking his mask. He landed on his back, threw his gun away and crawled quickly towards the exit. Another two or three paintballs hit him in the legs and back on his way out. I heard shots and several muffled thuds nearby - the teens sprinted towards the exit a few seconds later without their weapons. Cathy, crouched a yard from me behind the same barricade, looked over at me and raised her sausage claw as if to ask, "What do we do?"
"Cover me," I yelled, hoping she would think I had a plan other than making it to the exit without being hit. Credit where credit's due; she nodded, let out a guttural scream and stood up firing. A paintball immediately hit her in the neck, just under her mask, another ten or so struck her mask and chest. She went down with a thud, flailing and screaming and firing blindly. I took at least five of her shots to my torso, two to my legs and one to my groin. The paintballs hurt a lot

more than I thought they would, I'd expected a thud of sorts, maybe a light slap. It felt like being struck with a hammer and I screamed for her to stop. Another round hit me directly in the right nipple. I fired back.
She was a large target and I hit her ten, twenty, thirty times. I must have advanced at some point because by the time I ran out of paintballs, I had a knee on her chest. The lights came up and Simon ran towards us. He pushed me off Cathy and lifted her mask. She was sobbing hysterically, eyes wide and mouth open. There was a fair amount of spittle and a snot bubble made it to the size of a golf ball before popping.
"Did we win?" I asked.

Apparently Simon had to take Cathy to the hospital that evening as swelling from thirty or so point-blank shots to the neck caused breathing difficulties. They broke up a few months later after she slept with a white water rafting instructor while on vacation. Simon eventually gassed himself in his car.

"You wouldn't survive ten minutes at Ogilvy," I commented, "it would be like a chihuahua joining a wolf pack. They'd tear you apart the second you started yapping."
"The fuck do you know?" Ben spat, "I'd be the pack leader."
"There's no way your tiny legs would keep up on hunts. The others would have to carry you. In a little basket or something."
"Why would I have tiny legs? I'm one the wolves, not the chihuahua."

"I'd like to be a dolphin," Melissa contributed.

"Alright," Mike interjected, "Ben, get the copy done; David, shut the fuck up. You're not exactly the world's greatest employee either."

"Exactly," Ben sneered, then frowned.

"Anyone else have anything to add?" continued Mike, glancing at his watch.

"You know what would be much better than being a dolphin?" Kevin asked, "Being a killer whale. They eat dolphins."

"Anyone else?" asked Mike.

"Well," declared Jennifer excitedly, "I *was* going to wait until the end of the meeting... but..." She held her hands out towards the suggestion box like a 1950's television advertisement model, "let's have a look, shall we?"

Sometimes during production meetings, I like to imagine what it would be like if we were all marooned on a tropical island and had to survive. There'd probably be a lengthy discussion about a rock shaped like a frog on the first day, fire and shelter mentioned as future actionable items. We'd go to sleep cold and hungry but confident we had a strategy to move forward with. On the third or fourth day, we'd eat Melissa and that night, I'd stab everyone with a pointy stick while they were sleeping just in case I was next.

Shaking the box a little, perhaps to make sure the suggestions didn't come out in alphabetical order, Jennifer opened the lid.

There were eleven pieces of folder paper inside, which was a little disappointing as eight of them were mine. As if drawing an entry in a county fair raffle, Jennifer chose one at random and unfolded it.

"Okay, and the winner is, hahaha... *'There should be an inquiry into how it's possible to accidentally order 36 big yellow mugs instead of 12 t-shirts. It just doesn't make any sens...'* David, we've spoken about this, you need to let it go."
I was mildly annoyed that one of mine had been first despite the mathematical likelihood, "You said the suggestions would be anonymous."
Melissa slapped the table, "As if anyone else would write that, nobody else gives a fuck! It was three months ago."
"Okay," Jennifer interrupted, "let's move on."
She dug into the box and selected another suggestion, "Okay then... this is another one about mugs. David, how many of these did you write?"
Melissa slapped the table again, "What does it say?" she demanded.
"It doesn't matter," Jennifer replied, "we'll just ignore all suggestions made by David."
"That's hardly fair," I objected, "I may have included valid suggestions along with those regarding mugs."
"Did you?"
"That's not the point."
"We'll go on to the next one then... okay, this is just a receipt from a parking lot."
"Yes," Kevin said, "That's mine, I had to park there for a

client meeting so I should be reimbursed. Eight dollars for one hour is highway robbery."

"That's fine, but it's not really what the box is for... let's try another one... no, not that one..."

"Is it another one about me?" asked Melissa, glaring in my direction. Her lips looked like a Muppet's crease.

"Not this one either," continued Jennifer, "...ah, here's one... *'We should be allowed to use at our desks, not everyone likes the radio to have a radio on in the design department. It doesn't have to loud.'*"

"Ha! That's mine," Walter declared.

Walter once sent me an email, marked urgent, containing the words, 'Have you got because onions?'

It was a Friday afternoon and he'd left by the time I read it and replied with, 'Have I got *what* because onions?'

The question bothered me for the entire weekend. On Monday, I received the response, 'never mind tactics' and a few seconds after that, 'tictacs.'

"What does it even mean?" asked Mike.

"Headphones," explained Walter, "it was supposed to say, 'use headphones'. We should be allowed to use headphones at our desks."

Mike stared, "Well why didn't you write that? If we'd read the suggestion after you'd left for your doctor's appointment, none of us would have had a fucking clue what it was about. It's like a whole bunch of random words thrown together."

"But can I use headphones?"

"No you can't use headphones. This isn't the local skate park or a jogging path. If I need to speak to you about something, I'm not going to wave my arms about like an idiot to get your attention."

"I have excellent peripheral vision."

"I don't give a fuck if you have X-ray vision, you're not wearing headphones. Next."

"Can I go then?" asked Walter.

"What?"

"To my doctor's appointment."

"Oh, yes, fuck off then. What's it even for?"

"You're technically not allowed to ask that," Jennifer advised, "certainly not in a group setting."

"I don't give a fuck," Mike frowned, "it's like the tenth time he's had a doctor's appointment this month. Is he dying or something? Should we start advertising for a replacement designer?"

Walter rose and swung his bag over his shoulder, "It's just a rash."

"It might be Parkinson's," I suggested.

"Or shingles," added Kevin, "if you've ever had the measles then the shingles virus is already inside of you. I saw that on a TV commercial. The guy had a shingle on his face and it was painful to wear glasses. A black lady asked him how he was doing and he said, 'don't ask.' Have you ever had the measles?"

Walter frowned, "No."

"Well it's not shingles then. Probably just a rash."

There are a lot of commercials for pharmaceutical drugs on American television. Watching an episode of *Jeopardy* will subject you to at least twenty different advertisements featuring old people finally able to push their grandkids on a swing thanks to Ethdytrin or Apibatipopyol. There's so many drug brands that the marketing teams have given up bothering to come up with clever names and adopted the Scrabble bag shake, dump, and run with it approach.

"What's this drug do?"
"It stops dry eyes by reprogramming the part of the brain that controls the tear ducts."
"Any side effects?"
"Some people reported depression, loss of vision, paralysis and death, but we'll mention that soothingly in the commercial."
"Good. What are we going to call it?"
"Well, we were thinking Fsdfwjffdghrte. Keith came up with it when he had a stroke while typing. He's on medication that thins nose hairs."
"That works. And what's this one do?"
"The Olphystraxylzen? It's a once a month injection to reduce sun glare by two-percent. It's ready to take to market, we're just waiting on copy."

"Where is it?" Mike asked, 'The rash."
Jennifer quickly interrupted, "Mike..."
"Is it contagious?"
"Mike..."

Mike raised his hands, "Fine. But now we're all just going to assume it's on his penis. And contagious."
"It's only been two appointments," Walter declared as he exited, "and it's not on my penis, it's on my inner thigh. From riding." He closed the door behind him.
"Who goes to the doctor for a rash?" asked Mike, "Twice? Put some ointment on it. What's the doctor going to tell him? 'Yes, it's still a rash, have you been riding your bike again?' Perhaps stop riding your fucking bike. Buy a car you hippy fuck."

Walter denounces motor vehicles as a socially irresponsible form of transport. Unless he has to go somewhere that is too far to ride. Other people's motor vehicles are fine then. He won't offer to pay for petrol though because that supports companies who make dolphins sew sneakers for less than minimum wage. Walter's bicycle is made by Cannondale and he calls it 'the Cannondale' instead of 'my bike'. Apparently it's a decent brand but I'm not a bicycle rider so I don't care. If I'm on my way to work and see Walter riding, I drive past really close and sound my horn. Usually it just makes him wobble a bit but he fell off once.

"I own a bike," mentioned Kevin casually.
"You do?" asked Mike, genuinely surprised, "I wouldn't have pegged you as a bike rider."

Kevin isn't known for activity and complains of chest pains if he has to park his car at the furthest spot from the

.ce. People generally avoid asking him to help with
.ing as it means enduring a ten minute production of
moaning and groaning as he gets up from his chair. Even just answering his phone is like a Shakespearean tragedy performed in sighs. He's surprisingly active in an emergency though; once when Rebecca brought in tiramisu and announced there was only one piece left in the kitchen, he pushed Jodie into a potted plant to get out the door first. It was a plastic plant so it was fine. We just had to bend some of the fronds back in to place.

"Oh, I don't ride it," replied Kevin, "But I've definitely got one in the shed somewhere. I think it needs a new chain."
"They still make chains for Penny Farthings?" I asked.
"It's not a Penny Farthing," Kevin sneered, "It's a Schwinn. They make good bikes."

Schwinn do make good bikes. In particular, the 1981 Schwinn Stingray. Featuring red and yellow trim with banana seat and butterfly handlebars, it was marketed as *'that's not my bike, it's my Stingray'* so obviously targeted at Walter's demographic. I had a chinese knock-off of the Stingray, called the Stingerbike, when I was seven or eight. I tried convincing kids at school that the Stingerbike was a much better brand than the Stingray but nobody was buying it. The fake plastic gear shifter on the frame popped off when I did a bunnyhop and one of the kids brought a K-Mart flyer to school the next day showing it listed for $34.99, well short of my $500 claim.

"Schwinn do make good bikes," Mike agreed, "I had a Stingray when I was a kid. A red and yellow one."
"Very nice," I nodded, "I had the Stingerbike."
"Never heard of it."
"Similar to the Stingray. A bit better."
Jennifer shook the box, "Okay, next suggestion…"
She read it to herself, glanced at me, and screwed it up.
"Let's try another…"
Melissa threw her arms out in exasperation, "Oh my god! The website was confusing okay? It's not my fault they have a stupid website that doesn't make sense."
"Okay, but you had to type the number 9 in the yellow mug quantity box. Where'd you get the 9 from?"
"I take a size 9 in boots."
"What?"
"It's where the Zappo's box came from. Fuck you're stupid."

I saw a movie once, I can't recall its name, about an autistic child who cracks a code he finds in a puzzle book. I think his best friend was Bruce Willis but I might be getting mixed up with the movie about the child who can see ghosts. The puzzle book code turns out to be a telephone number, which the autistic child dials, and the guys who answer are really pissed at him for working out their puzzle. I think there was a chase scene on a train and maybe a fight with a shark but I might be mixing that up with one of the Jason Bourne movies. Regardless, the puzzle guys could have saved themselves a lot of fucking about by having Melissa write their code.

"How many more suggestions are there?" asked Mike.

Jennifer shuffled the contents of the box, "Four... and a button for some reason. Let's try this one... *'People should have to clean up in the kitchen if they make a mess. Otherwise we get ants.'* Okay, we've already covered that so let's go to the next one... it's just a post-it note with a drawing of cat."

"This has been a massive waste of time," Mike stated, "Was that you David?"

"The suggestions are meant to be anonymous, Mike."

"A drawing of a cat isn't a suggestion."

"It could be," I offered, "is there a question mark after the drawing of the cat? As in, 'cat?'"

"There is actually," replied Jennifer.

"Well, there you go. Cat?"

Jennifer screwed up the post-it note and selected another suggestion from the box, "Two left, let's get through these quickly shall we? Okay... *'Plastic plants shouldn't be in we should have we have lots of natural sunlight in the office.'*"

"Is that another one from Walter?" asked Mike, "Is he dyslexic? What's he suggesting? That we replace the artificial plants in the office with real ones?"

Jennifer re-read the suggestion, "I think so."

"Well that's just stupid, do you know how much those artificial plants cost?"

"There are no stupid suggestions, Mike."

"Bullshit. David proved that isn't true the moment he added a question mark to a drawing of a cat and put it in the box. Every suggestion in the box has been stupid. I say we take the hideous fucking thing outside and burn it."

There were cricket noises and a tumbleweed rolled across the boardroom. A prairie dog popped his head out of a hole, popped it back in again. A few of us glanced in Melissa's direction, other's avoided doing so. Ben's head stayed down but I could see his eyes darting left and right.

"Well, come on," continued Mike. He'd crossed the point of no return so plodded on, "baby heads on flowers? What the fuck? This is a branding agency, not Grandma Clementine's crappy arts and crafts store."

Melissa put down her pen and closed her diary. It was a deliberately slow action with at least double the impact closing her diary quickly with a soft thud would have had.
"Yes, well, some people like a bit of colour, " she declared, "and babies. I know I'm not a professional graphic designer but not everything has to be black Helvaletica on a white background."
"Around here it does," Mike asserted, reaching across the table to grab the box, "a client asked what this was yesterday and I told him it was a school project the cleaner's five-year-old child left behind... did you say *Helvaletica*?"
"Alright Mike," Jennifer interjected.
"It's okay," Melissa said, forcing a smile and waving a hand dismissively, "that's just his opinion."
"Yes," agreed Mike, "It *is* my opinion. An opinion supported by twenty years in the industry, nine awards, and the words 'Creative Director' on my office door. You're the secretary."
"Chief First Impression Officer."

Melissa was pleased with her latest title. Adding 'Chief' to the front of 'First Impression Officer' gave it weight and more accurately reflected her position within the company. It had the words officer *and* chief in it now and both of those words meant something. 'Chief Executive First Impression Officer' was the next step but she'd give it a few weeks.

"Please, it's the same thing. David, back me up here, is this not the ugliest fucking box you've ever seen?"
"Art *is* subjective."
"You fucking pussy."
"Mike..."
"No, I'm going to add my own suggestion to the baby head box," Mike stated. He waved an imaginary pen in the air, "Melissa is not to design anything in this office ever again, regardless of how fucking talented she imagines herself to be. And who the fuck said she could hang a painting of women holding umbrellas in the boardroom?"
He pretended to fold a giant piece of paper and place it in the box.

Mike tended to over-emphasise actions. He'd paid for acting lessons once after someone told him he'd be great in commercials. He only went to one lesson but learnt how to project digging with a giant shovel and mixing a giant cake to a stage audience. According to Mike, the acting coach said he was naturally gifted and had asked him to play the lead in an upcoming production of *Oklahoma*. He had to decline unfortunately, as it would have meant a lot of time off work.

Melissa pushed her chair back with a screech and stormed out, slamming the boardroom door behind her. She stormed back in a moment later, took the painting down, and left again without a word. We heard the front door slam and watched from the window as she crossed the parking lot and tossed the painting into a dumpster. It would have been more dramatic had it been a better throw as the painting bounced off the lip and she had to pick it up and toss it in again. On her way back, she glared and held her middle finger up towards the window.

"It's reflective glass," commented Mike, "She can't see in. What makes her think we're even paying any attention to her?"

The reflective glass in the boardroom is a constant source of entertainment. People regularly check their hair and clothing as they pass by. Sometimes people lean against the window and they jump when you bang on the glass. Once, a homeless man took a dump. Mike chased him off with a poster tube and Melissa had to wash the turds down a drain with a hose. The water pressure is pretty low at work so it took her about an hour. There was a bit of carrying on and a lot of dry-retching so we closed the blinds.

"You owe her an apology," said Jennifer.
"The fuck I do," replied Mike, "someone had to say it. And thanks for your support, David. I'll remember that."
"Why do I have to follow you down the rabbit hole?"

"Because you started the whole thing with your stupid suggestions. Oh look, there's one left in box, let's have a read, shall we?"

"That's probably not necessary."

"No, I insist. Let's see… *I suggest we never adopt hats made out of bees as the office uniform. It would be dangerous.*' Yes, I agree. Excellent suggestion. Hands up of all those in favour of never adopting hats made out of bees as the office uniform. Very fucking helpful, David."

I thought there'd be more suggestions from others. Boring suggestions about thermostat regulation or printing on both sides of paper to save ink. As it was Jennifer's idea, you'd think she'd have contributed at least one tedious suggestion herself. It's like holding a party and telling everyone to bring a dish but not bothering to make anything yourself. Then commenting that their dip isn't that great and they should try adding more paprika next time. Maybe use a nicer bowl. It had been a fairly successful production meeting though; I never saw the suggestion box again so at least something came out of it.

We wrapped it up after another brief discussion about ants, a lengthier discussion about puff-paint not sticking well to leather and leaving bits everywhere, and an estimate from Kevin on how many bags of Sphagnum Peat Moss he thought he'd need to buy for a 10'x30' garden plot. Nobody was in much of a rush to leave the boardroom because it meant walking past Melissa's desk.

We played *Rock, Paper, Scissors, Finger* to see who went first. It's similar to the standard game but every now and then you throw in the finger as your play. It gets a few chuckles and someone says, "Yes, okay, come on, just play it properly."

"You alright, Melissa?" I asked as I headed towards the stairs.
"Yes, of course I am," replied Melissa, "Why wouldn't I be? I'm just the secretary."
"Right. Oh, Jennifer asked me to give this to you." I placed the parking lot receipt on top of her monitor.
"Mm hm."
"I was just joking about the mugs."
"Mm hm."
"And I actually thought the painting wasn't bad. Good balance of light and dark. It reminded me of a Bob Ross."
"I've no idea who that is," she replied, "because I'm just the secretary."
"That's going to get old pretty quick."
"It was actually a paint-by-numbers kit."
"Really? You'd never have guessed."
"I know, right?"

I watched Melissa climb up onto the dumpster and fish the painting out just before closing time. My office overlooks the car park and I spend much of my afternoons flicking rubber-bands onto the roof of Ben's car. My record is 274 rubber bands and 18 pens but that was on the one day he parked almost directly under my window. She dusted the painting off and put it on the backseat of her Ford Fiesta before driving off.

Missing Missy

I'm not a big fan of cats. If I visit your house, I do not want to pat your cat, sit on the couch where it has been, or have you make me a sandwich after patting it. I didn't want that sandwich anyway. The Maxwell House coffee was bad enough and when you smelled the milk to see if it was still okay, despite being a week past its use by date, I saw your nose touch the carton.

I actually rescued a cat once. I was walking across a bridge, over a river that was in flood, when I heard mewing and saw a frantic cat being pulled along. I picked up a fairly hefty branch and threw it over the rail to where the cat was. I did not see it after that but I am pretty sure it would have climbed on and ridden the branch to safety.

From: Shannon Walkley
Date: Monday 21 June 2010 9.15am
To: David Thorne
Subject: Poster

Hi.

I opened the screen door yesterday and my cat got out and has been missing since then so I was wondering if you are not to busy you could make a poster for me.

It has to be A4 and I will photocopy it and put it around my suburb this afternoon.

This is the only photo of her I have she answers to the name Missy and is black and white and about 8 months old. missing on Harper street and my phone number.

Thanks Shan

From: David Thorne
Date: Monday 21 June 2010 9.26am
To: Shannon Walkley
Subject: Re: Poster

Dear Shannon,

That is shocking news. Luckily I was sitting down when I read your email and not half way up a ladder or tree. How are you holding up? I am surprised you managed to attend work at all what with thinking about Missy out there cold, frightened and alone... possibly lying on the side of the road, her back legs squashed by a vehicle, calling out "Shannon, where are you?"

Although I have two clients expecting completed work this afternoon, I will, of course, drop everything and do whatever it takes to facilitate the speedy return of Missy.

Regards, David

From: Shannon Walkley
Date: Monday 21 June 2010 9.37am
To: David Thorne
Subject: Re: Re: Poster

yeah ok thanks. I know you dont like cats but I am really worried about mine. I have to leave at 1pm today.

From: David Thorne
Date: Monday 21 June 2010 10.17am
To: Shannon Walkley
Subject: Re: Re: Re: Poster

Dear Shannon,

I never said I don't like cats. Once, having been invited to a party, I went clothes shopping beforehand and bought a pair of expensive G-Star boots. They were two sizes too small but I wanted them so badly I figured I could just wear them without socks and cut my toenails very short. As the party was only a few blocks from my place, I decided to walk.

After the first block, I lost all feeling in my feet. Arriving at the party, I stumbled into a guy named Steven, spilling Malibu & coke onto his white Wham 'Choose Life' t-shirt, and he punched me.

An hour or so after the incident, Steven sat down in a chair already occupied by a cat. The surprised cat clawed and snarled causing Steven to leap out of the chair, trip on a rug and strike his forehead onto the corner of a speaker; resulting in a two inch open gash.

In its shock, the cat also defecated, leaving Steven with a wet brown stain down the back of his beige cargo pants.

I liked that cat.

Attached poster as requested.

Regards, David

MISSING MISSY
A SHANNON PRODUCTION

From: Shannon Walkley
Date: Monday 21 June 2010 10.24am
To: David Thorne
Subject: Re: Re: Re: Re: Poster

yeah thats not what I was looking for at all. it looks like a movie and how come the photo of Missy is so small?

From: David Thorne
Date: Monday 21 June 2010 10.28am
To: Shannon Walkley
Subject: Re: Re: Re: Re: Re: Poster

Dear Shannon,

It's a design thing. The cat is lost in the negative space.

Regards, David.

From: Shannon Walkley
Date: Monday 21 June 2010 10.33am
To: David Thorne
Subject: Re: Re: Re: Re: Re: Re: Poster

Thats just stupid. Can you do it properly please? I am extremely emotional over this and was up all night in tears. you seem to think it is funny. Can you make the photo bigger and fix the text please.

From: David Thorne
Date: Monday 21 June 2010 10.46am
To: Shannon Walkley
Subject: Re: Re: Re: Re: Re: Re: Re: Poster

Dear Shannon,

Having worked with designers for a few years now, I'd have assumed you understood, despite our vague suggestions otherwise, we do not welcome constructive criticism.

I don't come downstairs and tell you how to send text messages, log onto Facebook and look out of the window.

I will overlook this however, as you are no doubt preoccupied with thoughts of Missy attempting to make her way home across busy intersections or being trapped in a drain as it slowly fills with water. I spent three days down a well once but that was just for fun.

Amended poster as per your instructions.

Regards, David.

From: Shannon Walkley
Date: Monday 21 June 2010 10.59am
To: David Thorne
Subject: Re: Re: Re: Re: Re: Re: Re: Re: Poster

This is worse than the other one. can you make it so it shows the whole photo of Missy and delete the stupid text that says missing missy off it? I just want it to say lost.

From: David Thorne
Date: Monday 21 June 2010 11.14am
To: Shannon Walkley
Subject: Re: Re: Re: Re: Re: Re: Re: Re: Re: Poster

From: Shannon Walkley
Date: Monday 21 June 2010 11.21am
To: David Thorne
Subject: Re: Re: Re: Re: Re: Re: Re: Re: Re: Re: Poster

yeah can you do the poster or not? I just want a photo and the word lost and the telephone number and when and where she was lost and her name. Not like a movie poster or anything stupid. I have to leave early today. If it was your cat I would help you. Thanks.

From: David Thorne
Date: Monday 21 June 2010 11.32am
To: Shannon Walkley
Subject: Awww

Dear Shannon,

I don't have a cat. I once agreed to look after a friend's cat for a week but after he dropped it off at my apartment and explained the concept of kitty litter, I kept the cat in a closed cardboard box in the shed and forgot about it. If I wanted to feed something and clean faeces, I wouldn't have put my mother in that home after her stroke. A week later, when my friend came to collect his cat, I pretended that I was not home and mailed the box to him. Apparently I failed to put enough stamps on the package and he had to collect it from the post office and pay eighteen dollars. He still goes on about that sometimes, people need to learn to let go.

I have attached the amended version of your poster as per your detailed instructions.

Regards, David.

From: Shannon Walkley
Date: Monday 21 June 2010 11.47am
To: David Thorne
Subject: Re: Awww

Where did you get that photo from? Thats not my cat.

From: David Thorne
Date: Monday 21 June 2010 11.58am
To: Shannon Walkley
Subject: Re: Re: Awww

I know, but that one is cute. As Missy has probably met any one of several violent ends, it's possible you might get a better cat out of this. If anybody calls and says, "I haven't seen your orange cat but I did find a black and white one with its hind legs run over by a car, do you want it?" you can politely decline and save yourself a costly veterinarian bill.

I knew someone who had a basset hound that had its hind legs removed after an accident and it had to walk around with one of those little buggies with wheels. If it had been my dog, I would have asked for all its legs to be replaced with wheels and had a remote control installed. I'd charge neighbourhood kids for rides and enter it in races. If I did the same with a horse, I could drive it to work. I'd call it Steven.

Regards, David

From: Shannon Walkley
Date: Monday 21 June 2010 12.07pm
To: David Thorne
Subject: Re: Re: Re: Awww

Please just use the photo I gave you.

From: David Thorne
Date: Monday 21 June 2010 12.22pm
To: Shannon Walkley
Subject: Re: Re: Re: Re: Awww

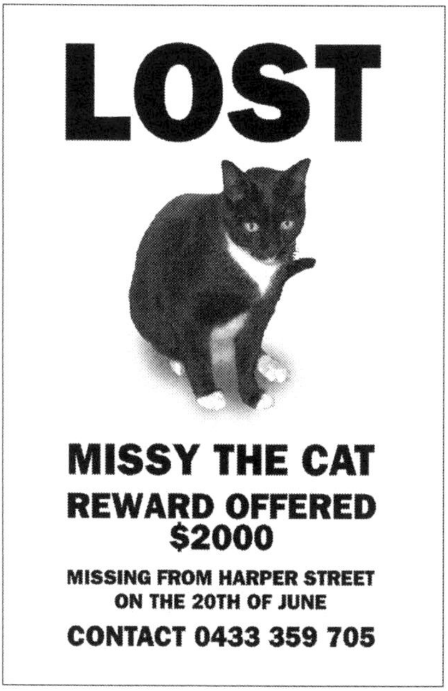

From: Shannon Walkley
Date: Monday 21 June 2010 12.34pm
To: David Thorne
Subject: Re: Re: Re: Re: Re: Awww

I didnt say there was a reward. I dont have $2000 dollars. What did you even put that there for? Apart from that it is perfect can you please remove the reward bit.

From: David Thorne
Date: Monday 21 June 2010 12.42pm
To: Shannon Walkley
Subject: Re: Re: Re: Re: Re: Re: Awww

From: Shannon Walkley
Date: Monday 21 June 2010 12.51pm
To: David Thorne
Subject: Re: Re: Re: Re: Re: Re: Re: Awww

Can you just take the reward bit off altogether? I have to leave in ten minutes and I still have to make photocopies.

From: David Thorne
Date: Monday 21 June 2010 12.56pm
To: Shannon Walkley
Subject: Re: Re: Re: Re: Re: Re: Re: Re: Awww

From: Shannon Walkley
Date: Monday 21 June 2010 1.03pm
To: David Thorne
Subject: Re: Re: Re: Re: Re: Re: Re: Re: Re: Awww

Fine. That will have to do.

Fire

There was a fire in the office kitchen this morning. It started in a toaster oven and lit the shelf above. It wasn't a very big fire and didn't cause a lot of damage but it was still quite exciting at the time; there was screaming and yelling and people trying to work out how to use the fire extinguisher. It hadn't been checked since August 1986 according to the label and made only a small 'pthh' sound when the trigger was pulled. It was Ben who eventually smothered the fire, with a wet teatowel, and he was quite proud of the fact.

"It probably would have set the entire building on fire if I hadn't managed to put it out."
"Yes, you're very brave, Ben. Like a tiny, shaved version of Smokey Bear. Tell us the story again."
"I didn't see you rushing to put it out."
"Only you can prevent office fires. Besides, you seemed to know what you were doing. I particularly liked the bit where you threw the fire extinguisher at it. Very effective. Now we have to replace the toaster *and* the microwave."
"You can't handle anyone else being the hero can you? Not everything has to be about you, David."
"Please. Who do you think is going to be remembered for the kitchen fire - the person who put it out or the person who started it?"

Tom's Diary.
A Week in the Life of a Creative Director

Hello, my name is Thomas and I run a design agency. You have probably heard of me as I am known as the Design Guru of Adelaide. Everybody calls me that. You can call me Tommy though. Or the Design Guru of Adelaide if you want. Just try it and see how it sounds. No? Ok, I wasn't asking you to call me that, I was just saying most people do. It's not a problem, Tommy then. Or the Design Guru of Adelaide if you say it a few times in your head and find you prefer it because it rolls off the tongue quite well. Okay, Thomas then.

Monday

10.30am

At work early this morning as I started writing a novel last night and am keen to check if any publishers have emailed me with expressions of interest yet. I am half way through and so far it is brilliant. It's about a guy who runs a design agency during the day but at night is a karate soldier with psychic powers. And he can fly and has lots of girlfriends. I'm currently looking through photos of me for an appropriate one to use on the cover. One that says 'creative genius' but at the same time 'hey'. I will probably use one where I am sitting on a chair as it will remind people of that statue of the guy thinking called Guy Thinking. Or the one of me on the beach as my hair looks great and I am not wearing a shirt which will sell books.

12.30pm

Have just ordered a new MacBook Pro as my current one is almost six months old and I cannot be expected to play Solitaire at these speeds. Staff complained about the speed of theirs when they heard but I spend four to five hours each day sitting behind them watching what they do and have witnessed first hand Photoshop running fine on the Macintosh IIci they share. I just upgraded it to 8Mb a few years ago and am far too busy to be dealing with their petty issues.

1.30pm

Spent the last hour writing another chapter of my novel. It now spans several millenia - from the nineteenth century to the twentieth - due to the main character being immortal. Having him first jousting redcoats then, later in the novel, time travelling robots, provides contrast and a break from the parts where he has a lot of girlfriends.

2.30pm

Have been sitting behind the staff having brilliant ideas. I think of things all the time that are brilliant. What is it called when you are a sideways thinker? I am one of those. I usually have about ten sideways ideas per minute. I should probably sit the exam for Mensa. I am just too busy. Just this morning, while shaving my back, I thought how great it would be if my shaver had an mp3 player built in as I was in the mood for a bit of Seal and that would have made the four and a half hour process more enjoyable. I'd call it the Rave'n'Shave.

3.30pm

Heading out for a drive to buy a kite as they are a great way of meeting new friends. I have a meeting scheduled but have told the secretary that if the client comes in before I get back, to talk about me and say, "I'm surprised you managed to get an appointment with him as he is in high demand and is known as the Design Guru of Adelaide."

4.30pm

Got back in time for client meeting, we agreed on a package that saves me 20% on local calls so it has been a successful day. Heading home as I am exhausted and Jumper is on cable.

Tuesday

12.30pm

Just got into the office as I was up late watching the movie *Jumper* and downloading the iPhone developer's kit. I played a lot of Space Invaders on my Commodore 64 when I was young and have a brilliant idea for an app that will make millions of dollars. It's a bit like Space Invaders but more like Frogger. With Braille touch screen for the blind.

1.30pm

Spent an hour writing another chapter of my novel. The main character now works as an international fashion model. And he has the ability to transport himself to any location on the planet as long as he has been there before.

2.30pm

As my creative energies are too large to be tethered to one discipline, in addition to becoming a famous author, I have decided to win Australian Idol this year.

I have my first singing lesson in half an hour. My voice is like one of those mermaids that sings to sailors as they crash onto rocks. But a man version with deeper voice and legs. Although I have the look they are after and perfect pitch and tenor, it makes sense to get a few pointers from a professional beforehand.

3.30pm

I've decided not to win Australian Idol this year, as I am far too busy.

4.00pm

Long day. Heading home after I send out an email to all staff reminding them to refer to me as the Design Guru of Adelaide and describe working with me as inspiring when they are talking about me with people at the pub or during family dinners.

Wednesday

11.00am

Late night. Decided to go to the pub and stayed for a few drinks even though everyone I knew left when I got there.

Guys are uneasy being around me with their girlfriends because they know she is thinking about me naked - probably lifting weights or dancing. Luckily, there was a girl at the bar by herself so I sat down and talked to her about me. Surprisingly, she had not heard of me even though I am very well known and people refer to me as the Design Guru of Adelaide. She had to leave before she could finish reading the news clippings about me that I keep in my pocket but she did agree to give me her mobile number, - 0123 456789 - so will ring her tonight and talk about me then.

1.40pm

Staff member just mentioned that eight years ago I said, "I have full body cancer with only one year to live and that's why everybody needs to work quicker." I told them that I never said that and to stop making things up. Anyway, I was talking about another guy who had cancer. He's dead now so they should show some respect.

2.00pm

Leaving early today to ring the girl I met last night. She will probably want to meet for a drink or come over to my place so I need to collate the photocopies of news clippings and magazine articles about me into a scrapbook for her and shampoo my chest. I also need to make a mix tape of my favourite songs. I know most of the dance moves to Disco by the Pet Shop Boys so will start slow with that before popping and locking for her with some Depeche Mode.

Thursday

9.30am

Early night last night. Walked into the office talking on phone, telling client I appreciate him for saying I was the most creative and brilliant person in Australia, when the phone rang. Explained to staff that my phone is one of the new iPhones that rings while you are on a call to let you know that someone else is calling and they just haven't heard of it yet because their phones are old. I got cut off at the same time it rang. That's the only reason I looked surprised.

10.30am

Finishing up the final chapters of my novel. It is now set in a post-apocalyptic future where the polar ice caps have melted, water covers the planet and people live in floating towns. The main character has gills on his neck and grows tomato plants.

11.00am

I have a meeting to go to in an hour and need to go shopping for something nice to wear as my green trucker hat doesn't go with any of my canvas shoes. I should start my own t-shirt company because I have lots of brilliant ideas for designs and people would be happy to pay upwards of two hundred dollars per shirt if they knew I had designed it. I'd sell them online and every time someone Googled my name, it would come up with my t-shirts and they would buy them. I should also make a website where people can buy my semen. I'm like one of those racehorses or a cow with award winning udders. I would do that if I weren't so busy.

4.30pm

Just got back from a four hour meeting with a potential client in regards to designing a business card for them. I'm very excited about where this could lead, as they are the eighteenth largest supplier of gravel in both the east and east-west suburbs of Adelaide. I will send them a quote in a few weeks as they take a long time to write.

I could tell they were impressed during the meeting, especially when I explained the need to incorporate cats into the design, as they continually rose, in a manner that can only be described as lengthy standing ovations, then sat down again when I kept talking. One of the female clients was very attracted to me so I spent an hour showing her colour photocopies of my Smart Roadster specs and explained what all the graphs meant. I will send her an email now and tell her my last girlfriend died of cancer so that she knows I am available, and will attach a photo of me sitting in my car. And one of me wearing jogging shorts so she knows I am athletic.

4.35pm

Heading home as I am exhausted both physically and mentally after two client meetings in as many months.

Friday

10.30am

Walked in and had an argument with Shannon. I don't see why I have to justify myself to her. It's my business and therefore my company Visa card. I do not appreciate being questioned. Obviously there has been some kind of mistake and we have been charged $29.95 per month by teenshemale.com in error. It's not her job to ring the bank and question the purchase when I told her I would take care of it even though I am extremely busy.

10.35am

Have put a password on my computer. Used a random selection of 128 numbers and characters so as to make it impossible for the secretary to guess. Will not write it down anywhere in case she finds it.

1.30pm

Completed my novel. It is the best book ever written and will become a best seller within weeks. This will mean that I will be very busy doing promotional tours and replying to people who have written thanking me for sharing my gift so I will need to tell my staff that I will not be here as often to give them the creative guidance they rely on me for. This will be upsetting but they have to understand that I owe it to my fans to do book signing tours and appear on *Dancing with the Stars*.

To celebrate the completion of my novel, I invited the staff over to my place to listen to stories about me but they all had prior plans.

Cloud Backgrounds

From: Walter Bowers
Date: Monday 17 August 2015 9.15am
To: David Thorne
Subject: Pay

Hey,

Did you know Jodie makes more per annum than me? Do you think I should say something to Mike?

....

From: David Thorne
Date: Monday 17 August 2015 9.19am
To: Walter Bowers
Subject: Re: Pay

Without question. I'm surprised you haven't already kicked in Mike's door and demanded an explanation. Apart from Jodie having worked here longer than you of course. How do you know her income?

David

From: Walter Bowers
Date: Monday 17 August 2015 9.25am
To: David Thorne
Subject: Re: Re: Pay

I just saw who gets what on Melissa's screen when she was getting coffee. I should be making more than Jodie the fat bitch doesn't even know how to use Photoshop. I've got a degree and she hasn't got shit. Mike's in a meeting or I would have. Should I just ask for a raise or should I say I know what Jodie gets and I should be getting at least the same as her?

From: David Thorne
Date: Monday 17 August 2015 9.36am
To: Walter Bowers
Subject: Re: Re: Re: Pay

Walter,

As you saw 'who gets what', you know that I also earn more than you - and a lot less than others who have been here longer.

Regardless, I think you're doing yourself a disservice by equating your worth to hers. Ignoring your inarguably superior set of skills, just having you around is worth twice Jodie's wage. However bad my day is, I can always depend on you to be having a worse one. Misery loves company and with you it's like a party. Just popping out of my office to have a quick squiz at your scowling sad head staring at the clock has gotten me through many an afternoon.

Feel free to ignore my advice but, if I were you, I'd demand a minimum of 20% over Jodie's current wage - unless of course you doubt your skills are 20% greater than hers. That way, when Mike talks you down to 10%, you still come out on top.

David

From: Walter Bowers
Date: Monday 17 August 2015 9.43am
To: David Thorne
Subject: Re: Re: Re: Re: Pay

I don't stare at the clock and I don't care that you make more than me, you're old. Jodie's not much older than I am. My skills are 2000% greater than hers. She doesn't know anything.

What if he says no?

From: David Thorne
Date: Monday 17 August 2015 9.52am
To: Walter Bowers
Subject: Re: Re: Re: Re: Re: Pay

Walter,

Why would Mike say no? If you provide a list of reasons - perhaps through a Power Point presentation - of why you deserve to be paid a fair amount for what you bring to the company, it would be illogical for him to anything of the sort.

I'd keep the list short, say five bullet points, to avoid repeating and diffusing your strengths. 'Misery party' is the same as 'Happiness vacuum' so don't use both. Focus on five defined strengths that you feel confident discussing further if prompted. It's pretty standard stuff.

Also, I'd strike while the iron's hot.

I know Mike has meetings all day but he breaks for lunch at twelve so that would probably be the best time to catch him. Do you think you could have a presentation ready by then?

It shouldn't take you long to set up the projector.

David

From: Walter Bowers
Date: Monday 17 August 2015 9.59am
To: David Thorne
Subject: Re: Re: Re: Re: Re: Re: Pay

Single screen or presentation?

From: David Thorne
Date: Monday 17 August 2015 10.04am
To: Walter Bowers
Subject: Re: Re: Re: Re: Re: Re: Re: Pay

A five screen presentation with animated page swipes and *boing* noises would obviously best showcase your talents but, as you only have a couple of hours, I'd suggest content and layout as priorities.

David

From: Walter Bowers
Date: Monday 17 August 2015 10.32am
To: David Thorne
Subject: Re: Re: Re: Re: Re: Re: Re: Pay

Something like this?

> **Why does Walter deserve to be paid more than Jodie??**
>
> - I have a degree in graphic design
> - I have experience in Photoshop and Illustrator
> - I work quickly
> - I can work unattended
> - I bring knowlege and skills to the company

From: David Thorne
Date: Monday 17 August 2015 10.38am
To: Walter Bowers
Subject: Re: Re: Re: Re: Re: Re: Re: Re: Re: Pay

Looks good.

I'd make the key words (paid, degree, experience, quickly, unattended, knowledge, skills) in bold as well though.

Also, change the dots to checkboxes and add another question mark.

David

From: Walter Bowers
Date: Monday 17 August 2015 10.57am
To: David Thorne
Subject: Re: Re: Re: Re: Re: Re: Re: Re: Re: Re: Pay

> ## Why does **Walter** deserve to be **paid** more than Jodie???
>
> ☑ I have a **degree** in graphic design
> ☑ I have **experience** in Photoshop and Illustrator
> ☑ I work **quickly**
> ☑ I can work **unattended**
> ☑ I bring **knowlege** and **skills** to the company

From: David Thorne
Date: Monday 17 August 2015 11.03am
To: Walter Bowers
Subject: Re: Re: Re: Re: Re: Re: Re: Re: Re: Re: Pay

Walter,

That's looking a lot better but when I said checkboxes, I had more of a chart thing in mind. A comparison between your strengths and Jodie's. The current layout allows one to question, "Yes, but which of these strengths does Jodie also have?" I'd make it a bit more obvious that she has none.

Also, as your five key points are meant to be strengths, not essays, I'd lose everything but the words in bold. The more simple you make it, the less there will be to explain.

The word 'quickly' won't work like that so change it to 'speedy' and change unattended to 'untenable' - they mean the same thing.

The word 'why' in the title is also a bit superfluous. The whole title is superfluous really.

I'd remove it and just have a large VS between your names. It will be a lot cleaner.

Also, if you wanted to push a point, you could have Jodie's name written in Comic Sans. It will add a subtle visual statement regarding her lack of typographic experience. That's up to you though.

David

From: Walter Bowers
Date: Monday 17 August 2015 11.08am
To: David Thorne
Subject: Re: Re: Re: Re: Re: Re: Re: Re: Re: Re: Re: Pay

Checkboxes like a chart?

From: David Thorne
Date: Monday 17 August 2015 11.12am
To: Walter Bowers
Subject: Re: Re: Re: Re: Re: Re: Re: Re: Re: Re: Re: Re: Pay

Yes, exactly. Unless you'd prefer a bar graph.

Also, add a cloud background.

From: Walter Bowers
Date: Monday 17 August 2015 11.35am
To: David Thorne
Subject: Re: Re: Re: Re: Re: Re: Re: Re: Re: Re: Re: Re: Re: Pay

Not sure about a cloud background.

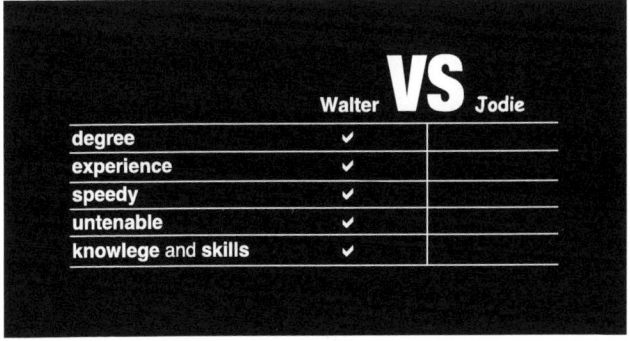

From: David Thorne
Date: Monday 17 August 2015 11.39am
To: Walter Bowers
Subject: Re: Re: Re: Re: Re: Re: Re: Re: Re: Re: Re: Re: Re: Re: Pay

Walter,

Mike likes cloud backgrounds and you only get one first impression.

One issue though, 'experience' and 'knowledge & skills' are the same thing so I would change 'knowledge & skills' to 'understanding' and change 'experience' to 'wisdom'. Also, change 'degree' to 'equipped'.

Once you've made these changes, it should be good to go.

David

....

From: Walter Bowers
Date: Monday 17 August 2015 11.51am
To: David Thorne
Subject: Re: Re: Re: Re: Re: Re: Re: Re: Re: Re: Re: Re: Re: Re: Re: Pay

I had to reverse the type because you couldn't see it otherwise. I haven't got time to make any more changes and I think it looks pretty good.

Walter VS Jodie		
equipped	✔	
wisdom	✔	
speedy	✔	
untenable	✔	
understanding	✔	

I could make the lensflare a bit brighter though.

From: David Thorne
Date: Monday 17 August 2015 11.53am
To: Walter Bowers
Subject: Re: Re: Re: Re: Re: Re: Re: Re: Re: Re: Re: Re: Re: Re: Re: Re: Re: Pay

I wouldn't mess with perfection. I'd say good luck but you won't need it.

David

From: Walter Bowers
Date: Monday 17 August 2015 11.56am
To: David Thorne
Subject: Re: Re: Re: Re: Re: Re: Re: Re: Re: Re: Re: Re: Re: Re: Re: Re: Re: Pay

Thanks.

From: Mike Campbell
Date: Monday 17 August 2015 12.37pm
To: David Thorne
Subject: Walter's timesheets

David, can I see you in my office when you have a moment?

Mike

Jumping Frog Fee

There are many things to be said for working in the design industry but as they are mostly negative, I'd rather write about robots. If I were a robot, programmed to serve people all day, I'd throw myself off a cliff. Working in the design industry is like being a robot. A robot that curses its positronic brain for not allowing it to ignore the first law and attach spinning blades to its arms and take out the next client that states, "that's nice but can we try it in green?" or, "Can you make the text bigger?"

Actually, scratch that, working in the design industry is more like being a whore. A dirty robot whore.

From: Robert Schaefer
Date: Monday 8 November 2010 9.11am
To: David Thorne
Subject: Artwork

Hello David,

Can you send me the artwork for our business cards you did last year. Finsbury Press has asked for the original files. I need the artwork before Wednesday so either this afternoon or tomorrow is fine.

Thanks Rob

From: David Thorne
Date: Monday 8 November 2010 10.24am
To: Robert Schaefer
Subject: Re: Artwork

Hello Bob,

I no longer work for that agency. Due to client account management resembling that German dance where men in tights slap each other, the company was basically trading insolvent and I resigned. While some may see this as the proverbial rat deserting a sinking ship, I prefer to think of it as quietly stepping out of a bathtub you have been sharing with four retarded children while they are busy arguing over who lost the soap.

I'd suggest contacting the agency and requesting your business card artwork before the owner swaps the art department computers for magic beans.

Alternatively, if you would like me to recreate the files for you, I'd be happy to help. I estimate this would take three hours at seventy-five dollars per hour.

Regards, David

From: Robert Schaefer
Date: Monday 8 November 2010 12.17pm
To: David Thorne
Subject: Re: Re: Artwork

It's Rob not Bob and I already emailed them and they said they don't have the files and to contact you. I'm not paying you $225 for artwork when I already paid you for the artwork last year.

From: David Thorne
Date: Monday 8 November 2010 3.02pm
To: Robert Schaefer
Subject: Re: Re: Re: Artwork

Dear Bob,

You paid the agency to provide artwork and I no longer work for that agency. While generally a frontline supporter of questioning logic, this support wavers drastically in the face of providing free work.

A few years back, I bought my first four-wheel-drive vehicle. The salesman who did the paperwork was named Roger. While on a camping trip several months later with my offspring, I parked the vehicle on a dirt incline near a river and set up camp. We awoke the next morning to discover it had rained, turning the dirt incline into a slippery mud incline, and our vehicle had slid roof-deep into the river.

Realising my phone was on the rear seat of the vehicle, along with our food, we rode a Coleman® inflatable air mattress down the river to the nearest town. It was a full days' journey and I will admit the thought of eating my offspring crossed my mind. This was less due to hunger than his constant complaining of, "Why do I have to hold on to the back while you ride?" and, "I can't feel my legs."

My offspring and I went shopping for a new vehicle a few weeks later. I did not to turn up at Roger's premises demanding a replacement vehicle for the one I lost. While it's possible Roger may have nodded, sympathized, and explained patiently the structure of modern commerce, it's more likely he would have just called me a dickhead.

Also, while three hours at $75.00 does equate to $225.00, the total cost to recreate and sent your business card artwork would be $450.00 due to the Jumping Frog fee.

Regards, David

From: Robert Schaefer
Date: Monday 8 November 2010 3.18pm
To: David Thorne
Subject: Re: Re: Re: Re: Artwork

I remember you from the meeting you were that idiot wearing a green Atari t-shirt.

Im NOT paying for work I have already paid for and 3 hours at $75.00 per hour is $225.00 NOT $450.00 - that is double. where the did you get double from and what the fuck is a jumping frog fee?

From: David Thorne
Date: Monday 8 November 2010 4.46pm
To: Robert Schaefer
Subject: Re: Re: Re: Re: Re: Artwork

Dear Bob,

I remember you from the meeting too (specifically your haggling over price and questioning why animated gifs can't be used on your business card) but no, sadly the Atari clad individual would have been Thomas, the owner. Nearing fifty, he feels retro t-shirts and trucker caps like the cool kids wear, disguise the fact. Once you've seen his size 40 lower-half squeezed into size 32 skinny jeans, like two parallel overflowing cake icing funnels, it can never be unseen.

I would have been the idiot wearing a suit and feigning interest in your business card requirements by appearing to take notes but actually creating an itemised list of things I'd rather be doing, starting with **#1**. Being shot in the neck with an arrow. Sometimes when I'm in meetings, I imagine I'm a robot programmed not to realise I am a robot and if the code word 'quantifiable' is mentioned, I will explode.

Other times, I imagine I am a small Indian girl collecting water for my village in a brightly painted clay pot.

The Jumping Frog fee relates to an event early on in my career when I made the mistake of offering a client a fixed price for a two-hundred-page website. Once the design was signed off and the build completed over a three-month period, the client requested that each page include a frog jumping around the screen because his wife liked frogs.

Purchasing a frog from the local pet store and filming it by holding a camera above and prodding it to jump, I spent the next two weeks incorporating it into every page of the website.

A few days later, the client described the addition as, "Very annoying," and requested it be removed and replaced with a 3D animated frog jumping onto the screen, holding a thumb up, and speaking the words, "Jump on down and grab a bargain."

After providing a quote for this, I was informed that the amendments would be made "under the original fixed price or no payment would be made at all." The next day, their home page was replaced with a single image of a frog giving the finger and a voice bubble stating, "I jump for cash, bitch."

After fifteen years in the design industry, I've realised the only difference between sitting in front of a computer facilitating client's requests and kneeling on a urine soaked truck-stop bathroom floor giving five-dollar blowjobs to men named Chuck, is the amount of urine on the floor.

As such, the Jumping Frog fee has evolved from insurance against post-project client demands, to client incentive to have somebody else do it.

Regards, David

From: Robert Schaefer
Date: Monday 8 November 2010 5.09pm
To: David Thorne
Subject: Re: Re: Re: Re: Re: Re: Artwork

You have until 10am tomorrow morning to send me the business card artwork or you will hear from my lawyer. I'm sick to death of dealing with you designers. Being able to draw and dressing like women doesn't make you special. You've got no idea who you're dealing with.

From: David Thorne
Date: Monday 8 November 2010 5.37pm
To: Robert Schaefer
Subject: Re: Re: Re: Re: Re: Re: Re: Artwork

Dear Bob,

That may be so but the label, "Some dick who wants free shit", doesn't require CSI profiling and while I'm no lawyer, I question testimony comprising of, "I paid an agency to provide me files, I lost the files, I now demand some guy who used to work there give me new files," would have much legal standing.

I also question your dissatisfaction with the price I have quoted as I believe the original charge for your work by the agency was around fifteen-hundred-dollars. While the actual process would have consisted of ten minutes on iStock.com for the background, two minutes pretending to consider a typeface other than Helvetica, and ten minutes putting it together, this is standard design industry practice and listed under 'Direction, Design and Build' on the invoice.

I do understand your objection to the established system of exchange of money for services though; I personally envision a utopian future where cash is replaced with interpretive dance. We agree on a particular style that seeks to translate particular feelings and emotions into movement & dramatic expression in exchange for groceries or business card artwork. And we all own jetpacks.

In a moment of stupidity, I once agreed to design a logo in exchange for yoga lessons. Contrary to what they would have you believe, you cannot actually embrace the sun as this would result in severe burns and your arms would need to be over one hundred and fifty million miles long. My favourite yoga move is the wiggly snake.

Unfortunately, until I can pay rent with mantras or grand eloquent movements in Spandex, I'll need cash.

Regards, David

From: Robert Schaefer
Date: Monday 8 November 2010 5.44pm
To: David Thorne
Subject: Re: Re: Re: Re: Re: Re: Re: Artwork

Fine. Send me the completed business card artwork tonight with an invoice.

From: David Thorne
Date: Monday 8 November 2010 5.49pm
To: Robert Schaefer
Subject: File attached:

ATT: David Thorne
RE: Invoices
DATE: Sep 14 2012

Dear David,

Last Thursday you were given the task of organizing Kevin's office birthday party due to Melissa being on annual leave. The budget you were given of $1000 was meant to be for catering. We assumed you would also organize CDs for the music.

I have checked with the accounts department and you managed to go over budget by $1155.25 which includes:

$375.00 1 day hire of inflatable jumping castle from Amusements Unlimited

$125.00 1 hour appearance of clown from Big Country Amusements

$125.00 1 hour appearance by face painter from Big Country Amusements

$85.00 1/2 hour appearance by mime from Big Country Amusements

$55.00 charge for helium and balloon animals from Big Country Amusements

$240.00 1 hour hire of Shetland pony from Big Country Amusements

$273.85 for pizzas from Dominos

$412.70 for cartons of beer from Murphy's Hotel

$230.20 for cartons of cigarettes from Murphy's Hotel

$33.50 Assorted party hats from Target

$200.00 2 hour hire of your niece Lauren to play music on her flute

$2155.25 Total

In future, if you are ever given the task of organizing events again, you are to check with the accounts department BEFORE you order and pay for any deliveries or services.

Sincerely

Jennifer Haines
Human Resources Manager

Telephones and Apps

Despite the fact that most agency account reps have never worked in, or have the vaguest idea about, the industry they represent, I like working with Kevin for exactly this reason. In the past year, he has asked me to courier him "a portable document disk", promised a client a new logo in exchange for 50% off the price of laying floor boards in his home, and once fell asleep during a client meeting. When I startled him awake by nudging him, he yelled, "The sprinklers are on!" but refused to go into further detail.

I've only ever seen Kevin lose his temper once. He was in a bad mood and I asked him if he had a piece of paper and a pen and he replied, "Do I look like a fucking stationary cupboard?" A couple of hours later, I discovered a ream of paper about twenty pens on my desk so he must have felt bad.

Also, despite having almost no idea what I am doing, part of my job role is maintaining the website - which somehow turned into fixing everyone's computer issues. Usually I welcome the break from real work, pretend there is an actual problem with their computer, and sit browsing their web history for an hour or so. While most people's web history contains some porn, Kevin's web history includes only paving techniques, caravanning tips, and, for some reason, mermaids.

From: Kevin Eastwood
Date: Thursday 19 January 2012 10.04am
To: David Thorne
Subject: Kotex artwork

Hi David,

I just tried emailing Jodie but got an auto responder that she is away. The client was happy with the last magazine ad layout and wants to place another in the February issue. Same info but different image. I said I would get a proof to them by tomorrow. Can you have a look at this for me?

Kevin

....

From: David Thorne
Date: Thursday 19 January 2012 10.32am
To: Kevin Eastwood
Subject: Re: Kotex artwork

Hello Kevin,

Jodie is currently away on stress leave but will be returning on the 23rd. Workload related stress is a leading cause of poor office productivity and a daily schedule of harvesting Farmville crops while eating cake and emailing people images of a cat wearing a tie stating, "I need everyone to stay late tonight, we really need to catch that red dot" apparently falls under this description.

While I would love to help, unfortunately I am unable to make amendments to Jodie's projects in her absence. This is partly due to not being the designer who undertook the brief, research, direction and development of the project, and partly due to Jodie password-protecting her computer after I changed her open Facebook page status to "Renting the *Die Hard* quadrilogy tonight. Yippee kayak, motherfuckers" while she was at a funeral.

In my defence, I thought she said she said she was going to a 'Food Mall.' Just last week Melissa stated there was cake in the kitchen and I heard a popping noise as air entered the vacuum Jodie's mass had occupied a nanosecond before.

Though I know her password, (it's her cat's name), there's little point using it. As Jodie has modeled her filing system on the Mandelbrot Set with files named 'qwedqwyer' and 'asdasydfg' several thousand folders deep, she will probably be back at work well before I manage to locate the file. I can leave a sticky note on her desk though if that helps.

David

From: Kevin Eastwood
Date: Thursday 19 January 2012 10.46am
To: David Thorne
Subject: Re: Re: Kotex artwork

Not really. You don't have to search for the file, it's 0396_kotex_click_advert_01.pdf.

It has the black panel at the bottom with the Kotex logo and info and the picture of the girls at the beach splashing each other. The picture and the quote just needs to be changed, keep the rest.

I fully realize Jodie worked on the account but when she's away other designers should have access to the files if someone needs them. Standard operating procedure. I guess having some kind of system in this place is too much to hope for.

Kevin

From: David Thorne
Date: Thursday 19 January 2012 11.01am
To: Kevin Eastwood
Subject: Re: Re: Re: Kotex artwork

Kevin,

We do have some kind of system and it's entirely hope based. Standard operating procedures consist of hoping nobody notices, hoping someone else gets blamed, and hoping account managers make promises only after checking the availability of sources to fulfill those promises.

Last month, while a file was in pre-press after a two day photoshoot featuring five babies for a Kimberly Clarke advertisement, you asked if it was too late to "make one of the babies Asian."

If you expect me to make amendments to the Kotex layout, I trust you have either a budget allocated for sourcing a replacement image that represents the confidence and resulting lifestyle benefits gained by using a particular brand of tampon, or have an existing 'rights free' replacement image in mind.

David

....

From: Kevin Eastwood
Date: Thursday 19 January 2012 11.09am
To: David Thorne
Subject: Re: Re: Re: Re: Kotex artwork

It's one photo change. It really isn't that complicated. Instead of girls at the beach, just change it to a girl riding a bike or similar and change the quote to something about being confident.

Kevin

....

From: David Thorne
Date: Thursday 19 January 2012 12.16pm
To: Kevin Eastwood
Subject: Requested amendment.

Attached pdf as requested.

From: Kevin Eastwood
Date: Thursday 19 January 2012 12.33pm
To: David Thorne
Subject: Re: Requested amendment.

Okay.

1. The photo looks nice but it doesn't have anything to do with tampons and the copy doesn't make any sense.

2. You cant even tell if it is a girl or guy and I didn't say motorbike. I said bikes.

3. If it was a cute girl on a moped or something like that that might work but not doing jumps.

Kevin

....

From: David Thorne
Date: Thursday 19 January 2012 12.51pm
To: Kevin Eastwood
Subject: Re: Re: Requested amendment.

Attached pdf with image change as requested.

From: Kevin Eastwood
Date: Thursday 19 January 2012 1.19pm
To: David Thorne
Subject: Re: Re: Re: Requested amendment.

I liked the first one better.

The couple look like idiots and the bike is too old. Girls like modern technology like telephones and apps. It's not rocket science.

Kevin

....

From: David Thorne
Date: Thursday 19 January 2012 1.46pm
To: Kevin Eastwood
Subject: Re: Re: Re: Re: Requested amendment.

Attached pdf with image change as requested.

From: Kevin Eastwood
Date: Thursday 19 January 2012 2.46pm
To: David Thorne
Subject: Re: Re: Re: Re: Re: Requested amendment.

I'll just send them the first one of the girl doing a jump and forward you their feedback. Thanks.

Kevin

....

From: David Thorne
Date: Thursday 19 January 2012 2.51pm
To: Kevin Eastwood
Subject: Re: Re: Re: Re: Re: Re: Requested amendment.

No problem. You may want to CC Jodie on that as I intend to be away next week.

....

From: Kevin Eastwood
Date: Thursday 19 January 2012 2.57pm
To: David Thorne
Subject: Re: Re: Re: Re: Re: Re: Re: Requested amendment.

Will do.

Charlie

From: Craig Buchanan
Date: Tuesday 14 March 2017 9.32am
To: David Thorne
Subject: Annual report files

Good morning,

Attached hi-res photos for Unilever AR you asked for.

Also, FYI, Walter was here for an interview yesterday afternoon. I saw him in Jason's office. He applied for the junior designer position we advertised in February. Trouble in paradise?

Craig

....

From: David Thorne
Date: Tuesday 14 March 2017 9.41am
To: Craig Buchanan
Subject: Re: Annual report files

Nice. He told me he was taking his dog to the vet. Thank you for the files. And the heads up.

David

From: David Thorne
Date: Tuesday 14 March 2017 9.46am
To: Walter Bowers
Subject: Vet

Morning Walter,

I hope everything went well at the vet's office yesterday. How's Charlie doing?

David

....

From: Walter Bowers
Date: Tuesday 14 March 2017 9.58am
To: David Thorne
Subject: Re: Vet

He's ok thanks for asking. just got to take dog antibiotics for a few weeks. The vet said it was probably just a virus.

....

From: David Thorne
Date: Tuesday 14 March 2017 10.05am
To: Walter Bowers
Subject: Re: Re: Vet

Walter,

Are you confident with the diagnosis? Someone told me recently that their dog was taking antibiotics for a virus but it turned out to be Prevaricate Pseudologia. I think you catch it from ticks. Did they test Charlie for that?

David

From: Walter Bowers
Date: Tuesday 14 March 2017 10.12am
To: David Thorne
Subject: Re: Re: Re: Vet

I think so. they did lots of tests and said it was just a virus.

From: David Thorne
Date: Tuesday 14 March 2017 10.21am
To: Walter Bowers
Subject: Re: Re: Re: Re: Vet

Walter,

It probably wouldn't hurt to make sure. Even a minor case of Prevaricate Pseudologia can get out of hand before you know it. One moment you're happily digging holes under fences, perhaps to get to greener grass, and the next, covered in tick bites and growling at hobos under a bridge when they try to take your blanket.

Which vet did you take Charlie to?

David

From: Walter Bowers
Date: Tuesday 14 March 2017 10.26am
To: David Thorne
Subject: Re: Re: Re: Re: Re: Vet

Just the vet near our place.

From: David Thorne
Date: Tuesday 14 March 2017 10.30am
To: Walter Bowers
Subject: Re: Re: Re: Re: Re: Re: Vet

Walter,

What's the name of it?

David

From: Walter Bowers
Date: Tuesday 14 March 2017 10.39am
To: David Thorne
Subject: Re: Re: Re: Re: Re: Re: Re: Vet

Its just called the veterinary clinic. why? the one on port road near the supermarket.

From: David Thorne
Date: Tuesday 14 March 2017 10.46am
To: Walter Bowers
Subject: Re: Re: Re: Re: Re: Re: Re: Re: Vet

Walter,

I'm quite familiar with that vet's office; it's where we take Banksy and Laika. Was it Doctor Wang or Doctor Richard who saw Charlie? Doctor Wang is young and new to the practice so it's possible she may not have the experience to recognise the tell-tale signs of Prevaricate Pseudologia.

David

From: Walter Bowers
Date: Tuesday 14 March 2017 10.58am
To: David Thorne
Subject: Re: Re: Re: Re: Re: Re: Re: Re: Re: Vet

doctor Richard.

From: David Thorne
Date: Tuesday 14 March 2017 11.06am
To: Walter Bowers
Subject: Re: Re: Re: Re: Re: Re: Re: Re: Re: Re: Vet

Walter,

You should be fine with the antibiotics then, Doctor Richard knows what she's doing. Her stature in the field of veterinary medicine is inversely proportionate to that of his height. Was it odd having a vet who is a dwarf?

David.

From: Walter Bowers
Date: Tuesday 14 March 2017 11.18am
To: David Thorne
Subject: Re: Re: Re: Re: Re: Re: Re: Re: Re: Re: Vet

no because I'm not predjajuiced.

From: David Thorne
Date: Tuesday 14 March 2017 11.29am
To: Walter Bowers
Subject: Re: Re: Re: Re: Re: Re: Re: Re: Re: Re: Re: Vet

Walter,

I wasn't inferring you were - it's just that Doctor Richard's dimensions, and attire, can come as a bit of a surprise if you're not expecting a three-foot tall transsexual vet - or three-foot-six if she's in high heels. Was she wearing high heels?

David

From: Walter Bowers
Date: Tuesday 14 March 2017 11.34am
To: David Thorne
Subject: Re: Re: Re: Re: Re: Re: Re: Re: Re: Re: Re: Re: Vet

how would I know he was on the other side of the bench that they put the animals on. whats your point?

From: David Thorne
Date: Tuesday 14 March 2017 11.47am
To: Walter Bowers
Subject: ally?

Walter,

I wasn't making one. The efficiency of a point depends entirely on it not being one the recipient wishes to avoid. I was simply enquiring out of concern for Charlie's welfare as there's been a lot of Prevaricate Pseudologia going about recently.

I get on well with Doctor Richard so I might give her a call and ask if Charlie was tested for it. If not, would you like me to book a follow-up appointment to get it done?

David

From: Walter Bowers
Date: Tuesday 14 March 2017 11.51am
To: David Thorne
Subject: Re: ally?

dont have to do that. ill juts antibiotics and if he doesnt get better than I'll take him back. Thanks though.

From: David Thorne
Date: Tuesday 14 March 2017 11.54am
To: Walter Bowers
Subject: Re: Re: ally?

Walter,

It's not a problem at all. Leave it with me.

David

From: Walter Bowers
Date: Tuesday 14 March 2017 12.02pm
To: David Thorne
Subject: Re: Re: Re: ally?

not that its any of your biusness but just so you know i didnt actually go to the vet yesterday. I just said that becasue I was embarrased to say that I hat to go to the doctor for a rash on my groin and Id prefer you didnt say anything to anyone.

From: David Thorne
Date: Tuesday 14 March 2017 12.09pm
To: Walter Bowers
Subject: vised story

Walter,

I'm disappointed you felt the need to lie to me but equally impressed by your 'smoke and mirror' deception. You're like the Uri Geller of absenteeism. No, I wont mention your groin rash to anyone. I hope it wasn't anything serious.

David

From: Walter Bowers
Date: Tuesday 14 March 2017 12.21pm
To: David Thorne
Subject: Re: vised story

no just from riding my bike. a friction rash. Ive had it before.

From: David Thorne
Date: Tuesday 14 March 2017 12.25pm
To: Walter Bowers
Subject: Re: Re: vised story

Walter,

Did they test for Prevaricate Pseudologia?

David

From: Walter Bowers
Date: Tuesday 14 March 2017 12.34pm
To: David Thorne
Subject: Re: Re: Re: vised story

no because Im not a dog. its just a rash. they gave me otment to put on it.

From: David Thorne
Date: Tuesday 14 March 2017 12.40pm
To: Walter Bowers
Subject: Re: Re: Re: Re: vised story

Walter,

What doctor's office did you go to?

David

From: Walter Bowers
Date: Tuesday 14 March 2017 12.47pm
To: David Thorne
Subject: Re: Re: Re: Re: Re: vised story

none of your busines.

Kevin's Retorts

Kevin, an account rep at the agency I work for, announced he is retiring next month. He turns sixty-five in January but doesn't look a day over eighty. I told him this and he retorted, "Please, you look like three raccoons wearing a corpse," then dropped a stapler in my coffee. Kevin has a penchant for dropping things in coffee. I've had pens, a mobile phone, a Pantone swatch book, and a hotdog in my cup. The larger items are preferable as I only find the smaller items after I've emptied the cup. Once I found half a box of paperclips in the bottom, which is paramount to attempted murder. While I won't miss having to guard my coffee after he leaves, I will miss Kevin's daily retorts. As such, I decided to document a week's worth:

New desk photo
"Is that your family, Kevin?"
"No Mike, it's someone else's family. I just knocked on their front door and asked if I could take a photo."

The kitchen
"Last one to use it should have to clean up their mess before the next person. It's just polite."
"Nobody asked about your weekend, Melissa."

Sandwiches ordered for lunch
"Are you really not going to eat any of them, Kevin?"
"No thank you, mayonnaise monkey."

Hairdresser appointment
"I'm thinking about getting it cut short."
"Good idea, Jennifer. Let me know if you'd like any beard grooming tips as well."

5.20PM
"You still here?"
"No, Walter, I'm a holographic projection. The real Kevin installed magic lasers in the ceiling."

Cat hair
"You're covered in cat hair, Kevin."
"I'd rather be covered in cat hair than your father's spit, Melissa."

Archive box
"Can I put this on your desk, Kevin?"
"I doubt it, Ben. With your physique I'm amazed you made it into my office without a lung collapsing."

Friday evening
"Doing anything on the weekend, Kevin?"
"No, I'll be in suspended animation for forty-eight hours, Mike. I've got a stasis chamber at home that lowers my heart rate to one beat per day. See you in an hour."

Kevin's Office

As it's Kevin's last week, Ben, Walter and I decided to help him clean out his office. Walter wasn't keen to participate but I threatened to tell Mike about a certain vet appointment if he didn't. Helping Kevin clean out his office entailed staying late a few nights, which is no small feat as I'm not a fan of being at the office at all. Kevin almost caught us once when he returned to the office after forgetting his keys, but we managed to throw his chair massager and coat rack out of a window and hide under his desk in time.

From: Kevin Eastwood
Date: Monday 9 October 2017 10.06am
To: All staff
Subject: Watering can

The yellow watering can from my office is missing. It's my personal watering can that I brought in from home to water my ficus and I'd appreciate people asking before they use my things. Please return ASAP.

My coffee mug is also nowhere to be found and I know it was on my desk before I left Friday.

Kevin

From: Kevin Eastwood
Date: Tuesday 10 October 2017 9.18am
To: All staff
Subject: Missing items

My watering can and coffee mug are still missing. I expect both to be located before the end of the day.

Someone has also taken all of my pens and whiteboard markers and I had stuff in my top drawer and now there's nothing in there except 1 rubber band.

There's no reason for anyone to enter my office when I'm not here. I will be locking my office door from now on.

Kevin

....

From: Kevin Eastwood
Date: Wednesday 11 October 2017 9.07am
To: All staff
Subject: THIEVES

I expect my office door to be put back on and my family photos returned IMMEDIATELY.

You picked the wrong person to mess with and just crossed the line. I'm filing a formal complaint with Jennifer and when I find out who's doing this, and I will, don't you worry, you're going to be extremely sorry.

Kevin

From: Kevin Eastwood
Date: Thursday 12 October 2017 9.08pm
To: All staff
Subject: FUCK YOU ALL

I don't even care who's taking my stuff. Without my desk I can't work so I'm going home. I'm not going to work on the floor. Give yourself a pat on the back. Good job, hope you're happy. Tomorrow's my last day so I expect my personal possessions back before I leave OR ELSE!!!

P.S. If one single leaf on my ficus is missing you are dead.

Kevin

....

From: Melissa Peters
Date: Friday 13 October 2017 9.32am
To: All staff
Subject: WHERE'S MY STUFF?

I'm sending this from Melissa's computer because I don't have one.

Thank god this is my last day as I've never had to deal with a more juvenile and inept group of halfwits in my life. It's like a day care service for mentally disabled children. You come in, walk around nodding and making stupid faces at each other, and then go home. Last month it took 2 weeks for me to get Inc. added to a brochure. 2 weeks for 3 letters and a dot. Just when I think the art department couldn't possibly get any more fucking useless, you put in extra effort and prove me wrong. Oh, and Walter, I'll be really disappointed if I find out you had anything to do with the theft of my possessions. The rest of you, not so much, you're all a bunch of dishonest, self-serving miscreants. And yes that includes you Mike and Jennifer. I doubt this company will last another year and when it folds, good luck finding work anywhere other than a public bathroom glory hole. You're less use than the talentless inbred monkeys in the art department, wandering around pretending you're doing something and calling meetings to ask what everyone else is doing. Breaking news, people: Nobody is doing anything.

I'm going to wait in the boardroom for 1 HOUR. If all my stuff isn't returned by then, I'm calling the police.

Kevin

....

From: Kevin Eastwood
Date: Friday 13 October 2017 11.22am
To: All staff
Subject: Drinks

Thank you for the cake. And for loading my car. Sorry about the last email. Looking forward to drinks this afternoon.

Kevin

Ben's Car

My car interior gets a little messy sometimes, everyone's does. Generally, when a vehicle is first purchased, it's cleaned out religiously for a few months, then intermittently, then when the console gets a bit cluttered with candy wrappers, receipts, lighters and notes. I smoke in my car so my cleaning schedule is based on how full the ashtray gets but if I have to pick someone up on short notice, I'll do the equivalent of hiding dirty dishes in the cupboard when people give you five minutes warning that they're coming over and shove the candy wrappers, receipts, lighters and notes in the glove box or center console, maybe give the dashboard a quick wipe with my sleeve.

This is not the case with my coworker Ben's car. Ben drives a blue 2006 Toyota Camry that last had the interior cleaned, I'm assuming, in 2006. An archaeological excavation of the layers is probably the only way to determine for sure but once, when he picked me up from the airport, I had to burrow with my feet to make room in the front passenger footwell and found a dead mouse - flattened like a pressed flower in a dictionary. It probably made its way in to feast on remnants of takeaway food and couldn't find its way out - or settled in and lived like a king on McDonald's fries and Taco Bell burritos until dying of old age. The rear of the vehicle is worse as you can only see the headrests of the back seats poking out. It's impossible to describe the smell as it's all of them.

Yesterday, while Ben was in meetings all day and I was procrastinating about laying out a sales brochure for window awnings, I decided to take the keys from Ben's desk and perform a 'stock take' of his vehicle. I made Walter, a junior designer at the agency, do the actual work as I didn't want to touch anything, but I gave him a pair of yellow dishwashing gloves from the kitchen to use so the complaining was unwarranted. Also, you'd assume Ben would have been pleased about it (two large garbage bags of rubbish were removed and items that might not have been rubbish were put in archive boxes and placed in his trunk) but he's been going on about 'invasion of privacy' for hours now and is threatening to file a formal complaint.

Regardless, here's a complete list of the contents of Ben's car:

16 McDonald's bags and 9 Burger King bags.
28 empty drink containers.
8 pairs of sunglasses.
12 various charging cables.
6 empty chip packets (barbecue).
2 empty Pringle's cans (sour cream & onion).
16 lighters.
11 unpaid parking tickets.
34 empty cigarette packets (Virginia Slims, Menthol).

760 cigarette butts (approximation).

2 Redbox DVDs (*Battleship* & *The Twilight Saga: Breaking Dawn Part 2*).

38 various takeaway food receipts.

1 sock.

8 scratch'n'win lottery tickets (scratched, no winners).

6 batteries (4 AAA and 2 AA, charge level unknown).

6 baby mice (flat).

3 empty pizza boxes.

1 piece of string (approximately 5" in length).

1 bird's nest.

46 compact disks.

1 panini-maker box containing a pair of boardshorts.

26 used napkins.

1 pair of tongs.

15 pens.

1 laser pen (confiscated).

1 Subway foot-long sandwich (contents unknown, petrified).

1 Fleshlight.

1 Wonderwave Fleshlight replacement sleeve.

1 box of kitchen backsplash tiles.

1 small notepad (green, contains handwritten poetry).

1 copy of Orson Scott Card's *Ender's Game*.

1 plastic sandwich bag containing marijuana (confiscated).

1 Stormtrooper figurine (4", confiscated).

4 unopened reams of A4 paper (suspiciously the same brand we have in the stationary cupboard).

And, finally, 1 box of Betty Crocker Super Moist instant cake mix (unopened, chocolate, expired in 2012).

Quick Logo

From: Eugene Buie
Date: Tuesday 26 April 2016 3.38pm
To: David Thorne
Subject: Quick Logo

David,

Hope you are well.

Do you remember the logo you did for the volunteer river cleanup last year? I was wondering if you'd mind doing a similar one for my church youth group. It doesn't need to be anything fancy - I was thinking maybe a dove. I'll leave it up to you though, you're the designer.

The river logo had hands making a circle with a water reed in the middle. Maybe you could just make the reed into a dove? That shouldn't take long.

I have a budget of $300 but that includes 2 banners. It's for a good cause and the group is not-for-profit.

No rush but it would be great to have it before the May services.

Yours, Eugene Buie

From: David Thorne
Date: Tuesday 26 April 2016 4.25pm
To: Eugene Buie
Subject: Re: Quick Logo

Hello Eugene,

Please find attached the revised hand logo incorporating a dove as requested. I feel it symbolises the church/youth relationship perfectly. It's in .eps format so will scale up well for banner usage and I look forward to seeing it in application.

We won't be billing you for this work.

Regards, David

From: Eugene Buie
Date: Wednesday 27 April 2016 10.05am
To: David Thorne
Subject: Re: Re: Quick Logo

Thank you, that's perfect.

Yours, Eugene Buie

Photography

I blame Melissa. She was the one who said, "I know someone" when the photographer we usually use was unavailable and his backup indisposed. Afterwards she stated, "Well I don't *know him, know him*, he took the photos at my sister's wedding. They weren't very good though."

From: David Thorne
Date: Wednesday 14 October 2015 10.55am
To: Robert Lawson
Subject: Patio photos

Hello Robert,

We received the flash drives this morning, thank you for couriering them to us so quickly.

I had Jodie copy the images over and we are both a little confused. Are these placeholder images? If so, when can we expect final photos?

In order to meet deadline, we require final photos by this Friday to have client approval before next Tuesday when the printers are expecting artwork.

Regards, David.

From: Robert Lawson
Date: Wednesday 14 October 2015 11.19am
To: David Thorne
Subject: Re: Patio photos

They are the final photos.

Rob

From: David Thorne
Date: Wednesday 14 October 2015 11.33am
To: Robert Lawson
Subject: Re: Re: Patio photos

Hello Robert,

Thank you for getting back to me so quickly. I've checked the proposal and it states the $3200 covers the "commission and delivery of professionally staged photographs."

The brief called for photos of a family enjoying year-round use of their patio - barbecuing, having a party, that kind of thing. The promotional material we are designing for the client is intended to be aspirational.

Twenty-eight snapshots of an overweight woman sitting in a chair provides little aspiration. Unless it's to have diabetes and what appears to be deep vein thrombosis.

Regards, David

From: Robert Lawson
Date: Wednesday 14 October 2015 11.58am
To: David Thorne
Subject: Re: Re: Re: Patio photos

Those are the only photos I could get. The photos were taken on a new Nikon D5500 which is 24.2 megapixel. You can't get any higher resolution than that.

Rob

From: David Thorne
Date: Wednesday 14 October 2015 12.17pm
To: Robert Lawson
Subject: Re: Re: Re: Re: Patio photos

Robert,

I'm not questioning the resolution. Being able to zoom in on an image while retaining sharp detail is hardly a bonus in this instance though. The model chosen looks like she is waiting at a bus stop on her way to spend Kohl's Cash. Probably on another pair of brown slacks.

Which photo would you suggest for the cover? The one of her raising her thumb or the one of her holding a slice of cantaloupe? Of the twenty-six remaining photos, seventeen show her sitting cross legged pointing at things and the other nine are blurry.

It was indicated in the first meeting that the price for photography included talent and props for the day, i.e. four adults, three children, cake and sparklers, food and wine. I don't recall 'grabbing Nan and sticking her outside by herself with a slice of cantaloupe' being discussed as a possible alternative.

What exactly did the $3200 cover?

Regards, David

From: Robert Lawson
Date: Wednesday 14 October 2015 12.41pm
To: David Thorne
Subject: Re: Re: Re: Re: Re: Patio photos

The $3200 covered camera equipment and my time. I took the photos and I don't appreciate you insulting my wife. People who are in their fifties build patios and most people just relax on their patios not have parties. It's about the patio.

The other people I asked to be there on the day had to take their dog to the vet to be put down and I didn't have time to organize anyone else.

If you want me to take more photos I can but I won't be able to get them to you before Friday.

Rob

From: David Thorne
Date: Wednesday 14 October 2015 1.12pm
To: Robert Lawson
Subject: Re: Re: Re: Re: Re: Re: Patio photos

Hello Robert,

Thank you for the offer but we won't be requiring more photographs of your wife - with or without additional sad family members.

We will, however, keep you in mind should we ever find ourselves commissioned to design brochures titled *Locating Backyard Items* or *Healthy Alfresco Snacks for the Lonely*.

As the $3200 agreed to was for the commission and delivery of professionally staged photographs, not to 'buy Robert a nice camera', I have notified the accounts department that we will not be paying that portion of your invoice.

We have, however, agreed to pay your $280 charge for 'burning' twenty-eight images to twenty-eight 128MB flash drives. Mainly because nobody knew quite how to react to the situation and Kevin in accounting said he can use the drives to send electronic Christmas cards to his friends and relatives this year.

Regards, David

From: Robert Lawson
Date: Wednesday 14 October 2015 1.26pm
To: David Thorne
Subject: Re: Re: Re: Re: Re: Re: Re: Patio photos

You have to pay the invoice in full for the amount agreed on. I'm out $2900 on the camera equipment alone plus travel and meetings.

You don't just get to say whether you pay or not after I've done the work. What planet do you live on?

Rob

From: David Thorne
Date: Wednesday 14 October 2015 1.52pm
To: Robert Lawson
Subject: Re: Re: Re: Re: Re: Re: Re: Re: Patio photos

Hello Robert,

You were present during the meeting in which we discussed project requirements.

At no point during that meeting did you put your hand up and ask, "How set on the whole 'family enjoying the benefits of year-round outdoor living' thing are you? I had more of a 'tuck-shop lady giving directions and handling fruit' approach in mind."

The fact that your fee covered the purchase price of equipment to fulfill the commission isn't reason to pay that fee but it does explain a lot. Is this your first camera?

Based on your business model, I'm considering opening my own surgery. I have no formal training in the field of medicine but if I order a stack of business cards with 'David Thorne, Professional Surgeon' printed on them and charge my first patient for a set of robes and a decent scalpel, I should be good to go. If questioned over fees after being admitted for an appendectomy and leaving with a pamphlet on toe fungus, I'll simply explain to them the 'out of pocket system' of business startup.

We have arranged for a capable photographer to redo the shoot on short notice. Project costs allocated to the commission and delivery of professionally staged photographs are therefore covered.

We will not be paying your invoice, recommending you to anyone, or listening to Melissa ever again when she says she "knows someone."

Regards, David

From: Robert Lawson
Date: Wednesday 14 October 2015 2.18pm
To: David Thorne
Subject: Re: Re: Re: Re: Re: Re: Re: Re: Re: Patio photos

If I haven't received full payment within 14 days, I'll be taking legal action.

Rob

....

From: David Thorne
Date: Wednesday 14 October 2015 2.29pm
To: Robert Lawson
Subject: Re: Re: Re: Re: Re: Re: Re: Re: Re: Re: Patio photos

Hello Robert,

If you need someone to represent you, let me know. I have a friend who could do with the cash. He makes very little as a Sandwich Artist so I'm sure if he can organise a briefcase and get someone to take his shift, he'd be happy to show up on the day and give it a whack.

Regards, David

From: Robert Lawson
Date: Wednesday 14 October 2015 3.04pm
To: David Thorne
Subject: Re: Re: Re: Re: Re: Re: Re: Re: Re: Re: Re: Patio photos

See you in court.

Who's Pat?

From: Mike Campbell
Date: Tuesday 15 March 2015 11.09am
To: David Thorne
Subject: Whiteboard

David,

Are you responsible for the drawing of Ben having sex with a toaster on the boardroom whiteboard?

Mike

From: David Thorne
Date: Tuesday 15 March 2016 11.13am
To: Mike Campbell
Subject: Re: Whiteboard

Hardly. I drew the image but responsibility for it still being there lies with whoever left a permanent marker amongst the whiteboard ones. Who does that?

David

From: Mike Campbell
Date: Tuesday 15 March 2016 11.18am
To: David Thorne
Subject: Re: Re: Whiteboard

Who draws a picture of someone fucking a toaster on the whiteboard? Permanent or not. Are you 10?

Mike

From: David Thorne
Date: Tuesday 15 March 2016 11.21am
To: Mike Campbell
Subject: Re: Re: Re: Whiteboard

Please. There's no way a ten-year-old would display that much attention to detail. I shaded.

David

From: Mike Campbell
Date: Tuesday 15 March 2016 11.27am
To: David Thorne
Subject: Re: Re: Re: Re: Whiteboard

Remove it.

Mike

From: Jennifer Haines
Date: Tuesday 15 March 2016 11.40am
To: ALL STAFF
Subject: Formal Notice

Att: All Staff.

Please be aware that producing illustrations depicting coworkers engaged in lewd acts is a form of sexual harassment and workplace bullying. It is a violation of the Employee Workplace Agreement (Section 4, Paragraphs 8 and 9) and will not be tolerated.

This applies to paper drawings, electronic files, whiteboard drawings and all other form of media. Furthermore, the boardroom whiteboard is visible by clients during meetings and is not there for your personal use or amusement.

Also, please ensure only whiteboard markers are used on all whiteboards in future.

Jennifer

From: Ben Townsend
Date: Tuesday 15 March 2016 11.48am
To: David Thorne
Subject: Suck shit

Suck shit. And if that's supposed to me it's a pretty sad reflection of your drawing skills because nobody would ever be able to tell.

From: David Thorne
Date: Tuesday 15 March 2016 11.51am
To: Ben Townsend
Subject: Re: Suck shit

The fedora is kind of a giveaway, Ben. Nobody else has worn one since 2011.

From: Ben Townsend
Date: Tuesday 15 March 2016 11.56am
To: David Thorne
Subject: Re: Re: Suck shit

Like you know fashion. 1992 called, it wants its hair back.

From: David Thorne
Date: Tuesday 15 March 2016 11.59am
To: Ben Townsend
Subject: Re: Re: Re: Suck shit

1766 also called. Your wooden teeth are due for a scraping.

From: Ben Townsend
Date: Tuesday 15 March 2016 12.03pm
To: David Thorne
Subject: Re: Re: Re: Re: Suck shit

That doesn't even make any sense. You did the joke wrong.

From: David Thorne
Date: Tuesday 15 March 2016 12.11pm
To: Ben Townsend
Subject: Re: Re: Re: Re: Re: Suck shit

The YMCA called. Your racquetball court is confirmed for 4PM.

From: Ben Townsend
Date: Tuesday 15 March 2016 12.15pm
To: David Thorne
Subject: Re: Re: Re: Re: Re: Re: Suck shit

Stop listening to my calls.

From: Walter Bowers
Date: Tuesday 15 March 2016 12.21pm
To: David Thorne
Subject: No Subject

Did you the whiteboard?

From: David Thorne
Date: Tuesday 15 March 2016 12.24pm
To: Walter Bowers
Subject: Re: No Subject

Can I buy a verb please, Pat?

From: Mike Campbell
Date: Tuesday 15 March 2016 12.31pm
To: David Thorne
Subject: Meeting

David,

I have a meeting in the boardroom at 2. I want the drawing removed before then please.

Mike

From: David Thorne
Date: Tuesday 15 March 2016 12.36pm
To: Mike Campbell
Subject: Re: Meeting

I'm not sure how. I attempted to remove the marker with Windex and a scourer but it took off more surface than ink. Ben's fedora is a bit lighter now though if that helps.

David

From: Mike Campbell
Date: Tuesday 15 March 2016 12.47pm
To: David Thorne
Subject: Re: Re: Meeting

No, it doesn't. Did you try nail polish remover?

Mike

From: David Thorne
Date: Tuesday 15 March 2016 12.50pm
To: Melissa Peters
Subject: Acetone

Melissa,

Do we have any nail polish remover? Someone left a permanent marker amongst the boardroom whiteboard markers and I need to remove a drawing of Ben having sex with a toaster.

David

From: Melissa Peters
Date: Tuesday 15 March 2016 12.59pm
To: David Thorne
Subject: Re: Acetone

You can't use nail polish remover. It will damage the whiteboard. You just have to rub a whiteboard marker tip over the permanent marker and it will come straight off.

Do you want me to do it for you?

From: David Thorne
Date: Tuesday 15 March 2016 1.03pm
To: Melissa Peters
Subject: Re: Re: Acetone

Yes please.

From: David Thorne
Date: Tuesday 15 March 2016 1.05pm
To: Mike Campbell
Subject: Re: Re: Re: Meeting

Mike,

I've spoken with Melissa. She says we can't use nail polish remover as it will damage the whiteboard. We're probably just going to have to live with it.

David

From: Mike Campbell
Date: Tuesday 15 March 2016 1.17pm
To: David Thorne
Subject: Re: Re: Re: Re: Meeting

No we wont. I don't give a fuck if you have to use sandpaper, I want the drawing removed before 2.

Mike

From: David Thorne
Date: Tuesday 15 March 2016 1.21pm
To: Mike Campbell
Subject: Re: Re: Re: Re: Re: Meeting

If you stand with your back against the whiteboard during the meeting, no-one will even see it.

David

From: Mike Campbell
Date: Tuesday 15 March 2016 1.27pm
To: David Thorne
Subject: Re: Re: Re: Re: Re: Re: Meeting

Is that meant to be a joke? Why would I be standing with my back against the whiteboard for the whole meeting?

Mike

From: David Thorne
Date: Tuesday 15 March 2016 1.40pm
To: Mike Campbell
Subject: Re: Re: Re: Re: Re: Re: Re: Meeting

There's any number of reasons why you might be standing with your back against the whiteboard. If anyone asks, tell them you have an itchy back and wiggle a bit while making pleasurable sounds. Tell them it's shingles. Apparently if you've ever had the measles then the shingles virus is already inside of you.

Alternatively, I could send Ben down to stand there. He's not busy at the moment. I overheard him tell somebody on the phone that he's bored and considering leaving early to play racquetball. I realise he's shorter than the height of the drawing but he could stand on a box. You can tell the client that he's on work experience and only there to observe.

Should I send him down at 2 or a bit before to practice?

David

From: Mike Campbell
Date: Tuesday 15 March 2016 1.48pm
To: David Thorne
Subject: Re: Re: Re: Re: Re: Re: Re: Meeting

Work out some way to remove the drawing or cover it up within the next 10 minutes please.

And yes, you can send Ben down. The only reason I'm having this meeting is because we've blown the deadline and if he's got time to fuck off and play racquetball, he can explain to the client why he hasn't even written the copy yet.

Mike

From: David Thorne
Date: Tuesday 15 March 2016 2.05pm
To: Ben Townsend
Subject: New product discussion

Ben,

Mike has asked that you be in the 2 o'clock meeting.

From: Ben Townsend
Date: Tuesday 15 March 2016 2.08pm
To: David Thorne
Subject: Re: New product discussion

What for? Who's it with? That meeting has already started.

From: David Thorne
Date: Tuesday 15 March 2016 2.11pm
To: Ben Townsend
Subject: Re: Re: New product discussion

Well you'd better get down there then. Have you heard of a company called Babolat? Apparently they make sporting gear or something.

Mike said to take down your racquetball equipment so he can get an idea of product dimensions.

From: Ben Townsend
Date: Tuesday 15 March 2016 2.13pm
To: David Thorne
Subject: Re: Re: Re: New product discussion

Alright.

From: Ben Townsend
Date: Tuesday 15 March 2016 2.45pm
To: David Thorne
Subject: Fuck you

Fucking liar.

From: David Thorne
Date: Tuesday 15 March 2016 2.48pm
To: Ben Townsend
Subject: Re: Fuck you

1070 called, it's still waiting on the Bayeux Tapestry copy.

From: Walter Bowers
Date: Tuesday 15 March 2016 3.34pm
To: David Thorne
Subject: Re: Re: No Subject

Who's Pat?

One Girl, Twelve Cups

Due to there being an unprecedented twelve coffee cups needing to be cleaned in the sink at work this morning, it is understandable that Shannon would be outraged by this intrusion on her Facebook and looking out the window time. Though kitchen duties may be an expected part of her job role, there is no reason why everyone should not reschedule work/client commitments and help out to ensure Shannon's social networking and looking out the window time is not interrupted.

From: Shannon
Date: Monday 17 August 2009 10.12am
To: Staff
Subject: Coffee cups

There were twelve coffee cups left in the sink this morning. Could you please wash coffee cups after using them.

Thanks, Shan

From: David Thorne
Date: Monday 17 August 2009 10.19am
To: Shannon
Subject: Re: Coffee cups

Morning Shannon,

My apologies. Those coffee cups were mine. I have a busy schedule today so decided to have all of my coffee breaks this morning rather than taking twelve separate breaks throughout the day.

I'm experiencing severe heart palpitations but am also typing at four hundred and seventy words per minute so should be able to leave early.

Regards, David

From: Shannon
Date: Monday 17 August 2009 10.31am
To: David Thorne
Subject: Re: Re: Coffee cups

I wasn't saying they were all your coffee cups.

I was just saying that I shouldnt have to wash twelve coffee cups when I don't drink coffee. People should wash their own coffee cups or at least take it in turns to wash them.

From: David Thorne
Date: Monday 17 August 2009 10.42am
To: Shannon
Subject: Re: Re: Re: Coffee cups

Shannon,

Perhaps you could construct some kind of chart. A roster system would enable us to work in an environment free of dirty coffee cups and put an end to any confusion regarding who the dirty coffee cup responsibility lies with.

David

From: Shannon
Date: Monday 17 August 2009 1.08pm
To: Staff
Subject: Kitchen Roster

Hi everyone.

I have discussed a kitchen roster with David and feel it would be fair if we took it in turns to do the dishes. I have put the roster in the kitchen so everyone can remember.

Thanks, Shan

From: David Thorne
Date: Monday 17 August 2009 1.22pm
To: Shannon
Subject: Colour coded coffee cup cleaning chart

Shannon,

I notice that you have colour coded the coffee cup cleaning chart. While I appreciate the creative effort that has gone into it, the light salmon colour you have chosen for my name is very effeminate. I'm sure you have not done this on purpose and are not inferring anything, but I would appreciate you rectifying this immediately.

Would it be possible to swap colours with Thomas as he has quite a nice dusty blue.

Thank you, David

From: Shannon
Date: Monday 17 August 2009 2.17pm
To: Staff
Subject: Updated kitchen roster

Hi.

I have changed David's colour to blue on the kitchen roster. Thomas is now green.

From: Thomas
Date: Monday 17 August 2009 2.24pm
To: David Thorne
Subject: What the fuck?

What the fuck is this email from Shannon? I'm not doing a kitchen roster. Was this your idea?

From: David Thorne
Date: Monday 17 August 2009 2.38pm
To: Thomas **Cc:** Shannon
Subject: Re: What the fuck?

Thomas, do you feel it is fair that Shannon should have to wash everyone's coffee cups? Apparently this morning there were twelve coffee cups in the sink.

I was planning to schedule a staff board meeting this afternoon to discuss the issue but Shannon has prepared a colour coded coffee cup cleaning chart for us instead.

We should all thank Shannon for taking the initiative and creating a system that will empower us to efficiently schedule client meetings and work commitments around our designated coffee cup cleaning duties. If at any stage our rostered coffee cup cleaning commitments coincide with work requirements, we can simply hold the client meeting in the kitchen - we can wash while the clients dry.

Today it may only be twelve coffee cups but tomorrow it could be several plates and a spoon. Then where will we be?

David

From: Thomas
Date: Monday 17 August 2009 2.56pm
To: Shannon
Subject: Kitchen stuff

Shannon, I don't need a chart telling me when to wash dishes. I'm not going to stop in the middle of writing proposals to wash cups.

David is being a fuckwit. I only use one coffee cup and I always rinse it out after I use it. If we have clients here and they use coffee cups then it is appreciated that you wash them as part of your job.

Thomas

From: Lillian
Date: Monday 17 August 2009 3.06pm
To: Thomas
Subject: Re: Kitchen stuff

What's this kitchen roster thing? Did you agree to this?

From: David Thorne
Date: Monday 17 August 2009 3.09pm
To: Shannon
Subject: Rescheduling coffee cup duties

Shannon, can I swap my rostered coffee cup cleaning duty this afternoon for Thursday? I've been busy all day and not had time to familiarise myself with correct coffee cup cleaning requirements.

I'm happy to reschedule my meetings to undertake a training session on dish washing detergent location and washcloth procedures with you if you have the time.

I also feel it would be quite helpful if you prepared some kind of Powerpoint presentation. Possibly with graphs.

Will I need to bring rubber gloves or will they be provided?

David

From: Shannon
Date: Monday 17 August 2009 3.20pm
To: David Thorne
Subject: Re: Rescheduling coffee cup duties

Whatever.

Simon's Pie Charts

I quite like Simon Edhouse; he's like the school teacher that would pull you aside after class and list, for an hour, every bad aspect of your personality and why you will never get anywhere while you nod and pretend to listen while thinking about how tight Sally Watts jeans were that day and wishing you were at home playing *Choplifter* on the family's new Amstrad.

I worked with Simon for a while at a branding agency named de Masi Jones. He was employed, as a business development manager, to bring in new clients yet somehow managed to be there for several months without bringing in a single one before leaving to pursue his own projects.

The lack of new clients may possibly be attributed to his being too occupied writing angry emails to other de Masi jones employees such as, "When I worked at Olgilvy in Hong Kong, everyone called me Mr Edhouse and said that I was doing a great job. Not once did the secretary there call me a wanker or have her grotty old g-strings poking out the top of her fat arse everyday making me feel ill."

Which I found much more entertaining than having to do the work new clients would have entailed.

From: Simon Edhouse
Date: Monday 16 November 2009 2.19pm
To: David Thorne
Subject: Logo Design

Hello David,

I'd like to catch up as I am working on a really exciting project at the moment and need a logo designed. Basically something representing peer to peer networking.

I have to have something to show prospective clients this week so would you be able to pull something together in the next few days? I will also need a couple of pie charts done for a 1 page website. If deal goes ahead there will be some good money in it for you.

Simon

From: David Thorne
Date: Monday 16 November 2009 3.52pm
To: Simon Edhouse
Subject: Re: Logo Design

Dear Simon,

Disregarding the fact that you have still not paid me for work I completed earlier this year - despite several assertions that you would do so, I would be delighted to spend my free time creating logos and pie charts for you based on further vague promises of future possible payment. Please find attached pie chart as requested and let me know of any changes required.

Regards, David

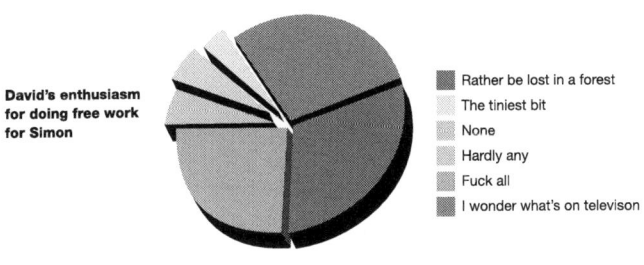

From: Simon Edhouse
Date: Monday 16 November 2009 4.11pm
To: David Thorne
Subject: Re: Re: Logo Design

Is that supposed to be a fucking joke? I told you the previous projects did not go ahead. I invested a lot more time and energy in those projects than you did. If you put as much energy into the projects as you do being a dickhead you would be a lot more successful.

From: David Thorne
Date: Monday 16 November 2009 5.27pm
To: Simon Edhouse
Subject: Re: Re: Re: Logo Design

Dear Simon,

You are correct and I apologise. Your last project was actually both commercially viable and original. Unfortunately the part that was commercially viable was not original, and the part that was original was not commercially viable.

I would no doubt find your ideas more 'cutting edge' and original if I had travelled forward in time from the 1950s but, as it stands, your ideas for technology based projects that have already been put into application by other people several years before you thought of them fail to generate the enthusiasm they possibly deserve. Having said that, if I had travelled forward in time, my time machine would probably put your peer to peer networking technology to shame as not only would it have commercial viability, but also an awesome logo and accompanying pie charts.

Regardless, I have, as requested, attached a logo that represents not only the peer to peer networking project you are currently working on, but working with you in general.

Regards, David

From: Simon Edhouse
Date: Tuesday 17 November 2009 11.07am
To: David Thorne
Subject: Re: Re: Re: Re: Logo Design

You just crossed the line. You have no idea about the potential this project has.

The technology allows users to network peer to peer, add contacts, share information and is potentially worth many millions of dollars and your short sightedness just cost you any chance of being involved.

From: David Thorne
Date: Tuesday 17 November 2009 1.36pm
To: Simon Edhouse
Subject: Re: Re: Re: Re: Re: Logo Design

Dear Simon,

So you have invented Twitter. Congratulations. This is where that time machine would definitely have come in quite handy.

When I was about twelve, I read that time slows down when approaching the speed of light so I constructed a time machine by securing my father's portable generator to the back of my mini-bike with rope and attaching the drive belt to the back wheel. Unfortunately, instead of travelling through time and finding myself in the future, I travelled about fifty metres along the footpath at 200mph before finding myself in a bush. When asked by the nurse filling out the hospital accident report "Cause of accident?" I stated 'time travel attempt' but she wrote down 'stupidity'.

If I did have a working time machine, the first thing I would do is go back four days and tell myself to read the warning on the hair removal cream packaging where it recommends not using on sensitive areas. I would then travel several months back to warn myself against agreeing to do copious amounts of design work for an old man wielding the business plan equivalent of a retarded child poking itself in the eye with a spoon, before finally travelling back to 1982 and explaining to myself the long term photographic repercussions of going to the hairdresser and asking for a haircut exactly like Simon LeBon's the day before a large family gathering.

Regards, David

....

From: Simon Edhouse
Date: Tuesday 17 November 2009 3.29pm
To: David Thorne
Subject: Re: Re: Re: Re: Re: Re: Logo Design

You really are a fucking idiot. The project I am working on will be more successful than twitter within a year.

When I sell the project for 40 million dollars I will ignore any emails from you begging to be a part of it and will send you a postcard from my yaght.

Ciao

From: David Thorne
Date: Tuesday 17 November 2009 3.58pm
To: Simon Edhouse
Subject: Re: Re: Re: Re: Re: Re: Re: Logo Design

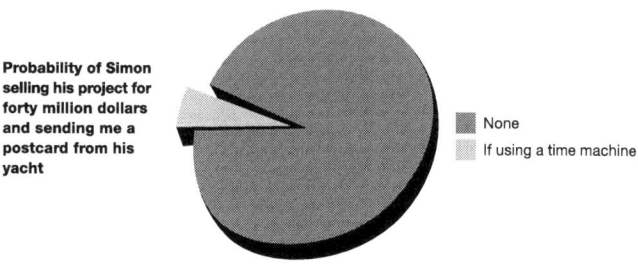

....

From: Simon Edhouse
Date: Tuesday 17 November 2009 4.10pm
To: David Thorne
Subject: Re: Re: Re: Re: Re: Re: Re: Logo Design

Anyone else would be able to see the opportunity I am presenting but not you. You have to be a fucking smartarse about it.

All I was asking for was a logo and a few piecharts which would have taken you a few fucking hours.

From: David Thorne
Date: Tuesday 17 November 2009 4.25pm
To: Simon Edhouse
Subject: Re: Re: Re: Re: Re: Re: Re: Re: Re: Logo Design

Dear Simon,

Actually, you were asking me to design a logotype which would have taken me a few hours and fifteen years experience. For free. With pie charts.

Usually when people don't ask me to design them a logo, pie charts or website, I, in return, do not ask them to paint my apartment, drive me to the airport, represent me in court or whatever it is they do for a living. Unfortunately though, as your business model consists entirely of "Facebook is cool, I am going to make a website just like that", this non exchange of free services has no foundation as you offer nothing of which I wont ask for.

Regards, David

....

From: Simon Edhouse
Date: Tuesday 17 November 2009 4.43pm
To: David Thorne
Subject: Re: Re: Re: Re: Re: Re: Re: Re: Re: Logo Design

What the fuck is your point? Are you going to do the logo and charts for me or not?

From: David Thorne
Date: Tuesday 17 November 2009 5.02pm
To: Simon Edhouse
Subject: Re: Re: Re: Re: Re: Re: Re: Re: Re: Re: Re: Logo Design

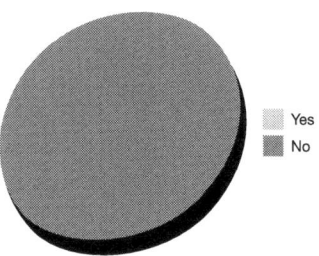

From: Simon Edhouse
Date: Tuesday 17 November 2009 5.13pm
To: David Thorne
Subject: Re: Re: Re: Re: Re: Re: Re: Re: Re: Re: Re: Re: Logo Design

Don't ever email me again.

From: David Thorne
Date: Tuesday 17 November 2009 5.19pm
To: Simon Edhouse
Subject: Re: Re: Re: Re: Re: Re: Re: Re: Re: Re: Re: Re: Logo Design

Okay. Good luck with your project. If you need anything let me know.

Regards, David

From: Simon Edhouse
Date: Tuesday 17 November 2009 5.27pm
To: David Thorne
Subject: Re: Re: Re: Re: Re: Re: Re: Re: Re: Re: Re: Re: Re: Logo Design

Get fucked.

Just a Sandwich, Thanks

I don't use Microsoft Word. As a designer and Mac user, the only time I ever open Word is when some idiot sends me an attachment in Word format. Melissa once emailed me a copy of an email as a word document. The document contained a screenshot of the original email. I'm deleting Word from my computer after I finish writing this line.

Also, Melissa's favourite movie is *Twilight*, which explains a lot. I was actually at the cinema while *Twilight* was showing (to watch a different movie not featuring sparkly vampires) and ordered a large coke. Not realizing I was expected to select between two *Twilight* branded plastic cups, when I was asked, "Team Edward or Team Jacob?" I replied, "Team couldn't care less" and was given a *Sex in the City* cup. Given a choice between a movie about four middle aged women discussing shoes or one about riding piggy-back through forests, I would just pick the shortest.

From: Melissa Peters
Date: Monday 27 February 2012 9.38am
To: All staff
Subject: Form

Hi everyone,

I know your really busy this week trying to get the annual report layout done on time so I will get everyone their lunches this week and bring them back instead of everyone having to go to the shops themselves. Theres a lunch order form attached in Word format. Just print it out and write down what you want and leave it on my desk. I'll write in the price when I am at the shops and at the end of the week i'll work out your total and what you owe petty cash.

Thanks Mel

From: David Thorne
Date: Monday 27 February 2012 9.47am
To: Melissa Peters
Subject: Re: Form

Melissa,

While I appreciate your efforts to improve productivity by removing the only half hour reprieve I get each day, couldn't I just tell you what I want and you write it down?

David

From: Melissa Peters
Date: Monday 27 February 2012 9.54am
To: David Thorne
Subject: Re: Re: Form

No because then I would have to write everyones down. Its quicker if you all do it yourselves.

Mel

From: David Thorne
Date: Monday 27 February 2012 9.57am
To: Melissa Peters
Subject: Re: Re: Re: Form

How long did it take you to make the form in Word?

....

From: Melissa Peters
Date: Monday 27 February 2012 10.02am
To: David Thorne
Subject: Re: Re: Re: Re: Form

Can you just fill it out please?

....

From: David Thorne
Date: Monday 27 February 2012 10.42am
To: Melissa Peters
Subject: Re: Re: Re: Re: Re: Form

Please find the order form attached. I thought it would be quicker to scan and attach as a password protected .RAR file than put it on your desk. The password is Fritter.

I apologise for the delay getting it back to you, I don't use Word so I had to learn Word. I'll mark the forty minutes down on my time sheet as Melissalaneous.

David

LUNCH ORDER FORM

NAME David Thorne

DATE 27 / 02 / 2012

ORDER	PRICE:
Milk	
Bread	
Confetti	
Mayonaise (Kraft original)	
Pickles	
Window cleaner	
Butter	
Tomatoes	
Oven Mittens	
Basil	
Mozarella cheese	
Beer	
Keurig K-cups (Black Tiger by Coffee People)	
Chips	
A t-shirt with a dragon on it	
Sour cream	
TOTAL	

From: Melissa Peters
Date: Monday 27 February 2012 10.51am
To: David Thorne
Subject: Re: Re: Re: Re: Re: Re: Form

I'm not doing your shopping for you and you're not meant to scan it back in and email it to me. If you email it to me I just have to print it out. The form is for lunch from the deli down the road. Just things from there. They have sandwiches.

Mel

From: David Thorne
Date: Monday 27 February 2012 10.56am
To: Melissa Peters
Subject: Re: Re: Re: Re: Re: Re: Re: Form

I'll just have a sandwich then.

From: Melissa Peters
Date: Monday 27 February 2012 11.02am
To: David Thorne
Subject: Re: Re: Re: Re: Re: Re: Re: Form

Then write it on the form. That's the whole point of it. Why is it so confusing for you? Everyone else has filled out theirs.

Mel

LUNCH ORDER FORM

NAME   David Thorne

DATE   27 / 02 / 2012

ORDER   Just a sandwich thanks.

From: Melissa Peters
Date: Monday 27 February 2012 11.41am
To: David Thorne
Subject: Re: Attached order in .EPS format

What kind of sandwich? I'm not a mind reader. Everyone else wrote down exactly what they want. I'm doing this to help you you know. I'm going out at 12.30.

....

From: David Thorne
Date: Monday 27 February 2012 11.46am
To: Melissa Peters
Subject: Re: Re: Attached order in .EPS format

Nice day for it. I'd probably pop out myself if I weren't so busy with all these forms. If you're going anywhere near a hardware store, could you get me a key cut? For anywhere, I don't mind.

....

From: Melissa Peters
Date: Monday 27 February 2012 11.55am
To: David Thorne
Subject: Re: Re: Re: Attached order in .EPS format

Im not going to a hardware store. Do you want something for lunch or not? And if you just write I want a sandwich or whatever dumb shit you want without being exact then I'm not getting you anything.

LUNCH ORDER FORM

NAME David Thorne

DATE 27 / 02 / 2012

ORDER 1 x Sandwich. **PRICE:**

The sandwich should consist of two slices of fresh white bread (a) and (b), with the following produce inbetween:
(c) 1 x slice of swiss cheese
(d) 8 x shakes of pepper
(e) 1 x thin slice of tomato
(f) 1 x small amount of butter per inward facing surface of each slice of bread.

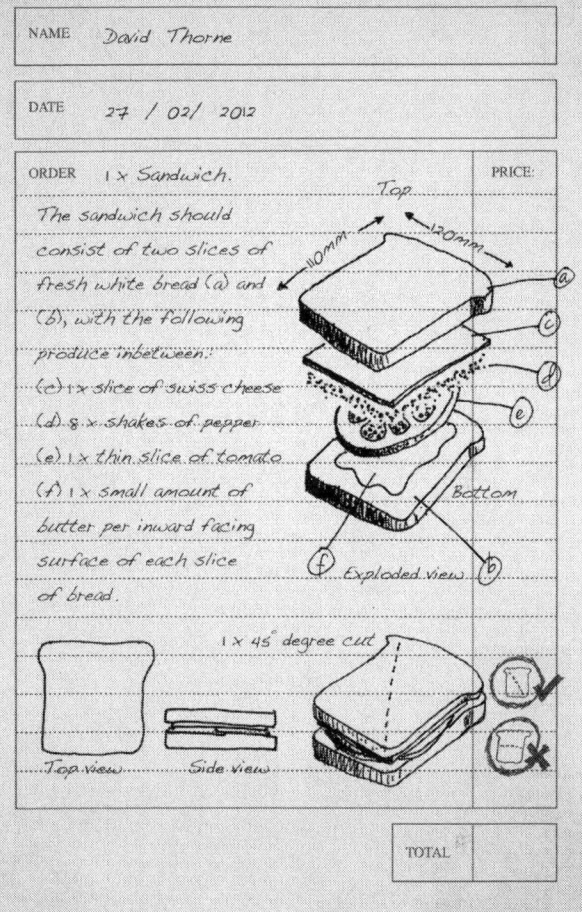

TOTAL

About the Author

Thorne was born in 1854 in the British colony of Victoria, Australia, as the third of eight children to Irish parents. His father, a transported convict, died shortly after serving a six-month prison sentence, leaving David, then aged 12, as the eldest male of the household. The Thorne's were a poor family who saw themselves as downtrodden by the Squattocracy and as victims of police persecution. While a teenager, David served a three-year prison term for receiving a stolen horse.

A violent confrontation over a wood-chopping license occurred at the Thorne family's home in 1878, and David shot dead three policemen. The Government of Victoria proclaimed him an outlaw.

David eluded the police for two years, thanks in part to the support of an extensive network of sympathisers. During that time, Thorne robbed dozens of banks, government offices, and police stations. In a manifesto letter, David - denouncing the police, the Victorian government and the British Empire - set down his own account of the events leading up to his outlawry. Demanding justice for his family and the rural poor, he threatened dire consequences against those who defied him.

In 1880, Thorne attempted to derail and ambush a police train but failed. He escaped but an informant told the police where he was hiding and, the following morning, they surrounded the house and called for Thorne to surrender.

Thorne, heavily armed and wearing quarter-inch-thick head and body metal armour fashioned from stolen ploughs, stepped out of the house and engaged in a gun battle with the police. Several members of the scattered police line were killed. Many returned fire but to no effect as Thorne walked steadily towards them; advancing fifty or so yards until being shot in the knee. He collapsed and yelled, "I'm done!" but when an officer went to disarm him, Thorne used his last bullet to shoot the policeman in the face. Several officers then rushed Thorne and he was captured.

Thorne was tried, convicted and sentenced to death by hanging, which was carried out at the Old Melbourne Gaol. His last words were, "Such is life".

Made in the USA
Columbia, SC
28 June 2019